The
Embroidery Design
Sourcebook

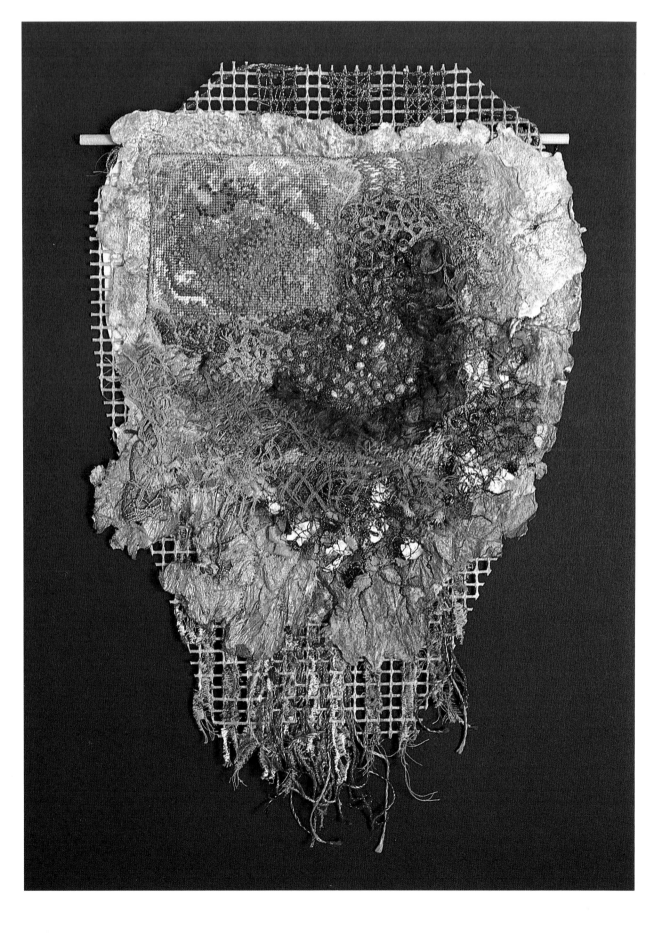

The Embroidery Design Sourcebook

Inspiration from around the world

HELEN FAIRFIELD

Photographs by
Peter Haines

CASSELL

A CASSELL BOOK

First published in the UK
1994 by Cassell
Villiers House
41/47 Strand
London
WC2N 5JE

Distributed in the United States
by Sterling Publishing Co., Inc.
387 Park Avenue South, New York, NY 10016-8810

Distributed in Australia
by Capricorn Link (Australia) Pty Ltd
2/13 Carrington Road, Castle Hill, NSW 2154

British Library Cataloguing-in-Publication Data
A catalogue record for this book is available from the British Library

ISBN 0-304-34199-1

Typeset by Litho Link Ltd, Welshpool, Powys, Wales

Printed and bound in Slovenia by Printing house Ljudska pravica
by arrangement with Korotan Italiana, Ljubljana
All illustrations and embroideries by the author except where otherwise stated

FRONTISPIECE *Panel based on the Alhambra Vase in
the Museo del Arte, Granada*

Contents

Introduction

The urge to decorate oneself and one's surroundings seems to be innate in the human race. While some primitive peoples mixed animal fats with pounded earth to paint the walls of caves, or laboriously engraved lines into the smooth surfaces of bone, others pricked their own flesh in patterns and rubbed coloured inks into the punctures to make permanent the designs so pleasing to themselves (or frightening to their enemies). Some peoples wove baskets of reeds or withies, decorating them by varying the colours of the stalks and the patterns used. Others incised clay pots with a pattern, or decorated them with liquid slip made by mixing a contrasting shade of clay with water.

Each emerging civilization evolved its own style of decoration. Because the images produced were based on natural objects, or on the geometrical shapes achieved by the interaction of such things as the straight strips of bark used in weaving or the circular clay coils of a pot, similar shapes were produced by peoples widely separated geographically; nevertheless each culture evolved a style special to itself.

Embroidery was doubtless one of the early arts in which these styles were displayed, but its very perishability means that few examples have survived more than a thousand years. Our knowledge of the techniques and materials available to the older civilizations therefore has to be gleaned from their interpretations in paintings, mosaics and carvings.

It is not too important for the modern embroiderer to know what stitches the Babylonians used, or whether blackwork embroidery was indeed known in the Egypt of the Pharaohs, though such knowledge might add to our pleasure in the subject. We possess an impressive vocabulary of techniques from our heritage of the past millennium, or borrowed from other cultures in this rapidly shrinking world, with which to interpret their designs.

The purpose of this book is to introduce the embroiderer to historical sources of design with which she (or he) may be unfamiliar, and to suggest possible methods of interpretation. Where possible, the techniques in which the designs were worked are also outlined.

Because some subjects remain of constant interest, I have tried to show how the treatment of a few of them has changed through the ages and across the world. As an example, the illustration on p.7 shows the varying treatment of the grapevine over several thousand years.

I have assumed that readers will have a basic grounding in simple embroidery techniques. In each chapter, however, at least one method of interpretation will be touched upon.

On p.124 you will find a list of books to help you with your pursuit of the many aspects of embroidery, and to extend your personal study of the design sources to which I am about to introduce you.

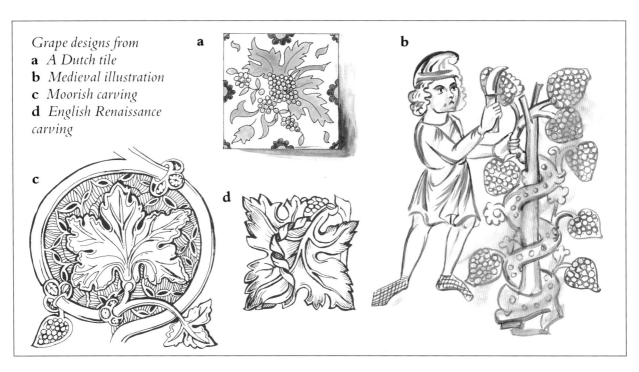

Grape designs from
a *A Dutch tile*
b *Medieval illustration*
c *Moorish carving*
d *English Renaissance carving*

a

b

c

d

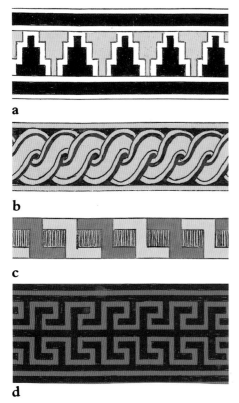

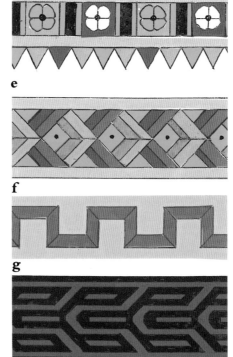

a

b

c

d

e

f

g

h

Geometrical forms from all over the world
a *Painted ornament from Nimrud*
b *Ornament from Isphahan, Persia*
c *Mexican pottery in the British Museum*
d *Greek decoration from the ceiling of the Propylaea*
e *Pattern from a mummy case in the Louvre*
f *Border from a medieval manuscript*
g *Carving from around a Norman church door*
h *Ornament from eighteenth-century Italian majolica (tin-glazed pottery)*

METHODS AND MATERIALS

Interpreting the rules

Many well-meaning people (most of whom are not embroiderers) will tell you that there is a right and a wrong way to approach each type of embroidery, and to work each separate stitch. You will find books demanding that you use methods which have been evolved over the centuries. Whilst it is advisable for beginners to follow these rules so as to avoid falling into bad habits, do remember that embroidery is a medium of expression – the rules are there as a foundation to your work, not as a prison to confine your imagination.

So use your common sense. If you are embroidering a cushion, use a foundation and threads which will wear well, base fabrics and threads which respond to common methods of cleaning, and decoration which will not catch on people's clothing nor be sharp to sit against. If you are working on a panel to be displayed under glass, on the other hand, you can use the materials, decoration and methods which best suit your interpretation of the subject, because considerations of wear and cleaning are not important here.

The only rule which should never be broken is always to use the best materials you can afford, even when you are just starting. It is maddening to find that you have expended infinite pains on a piece of work which will never look good when completed because the materials were inferior, or which will pull out of shape because the basic fabric is too flimsy to carry the embroidery.

Frames

Working fabric loosely in your hand may feel comfortable, but it will probably add considerably to your problems – it is difficult, for instance, to control tension without using a frame. The size and type of frame will depend

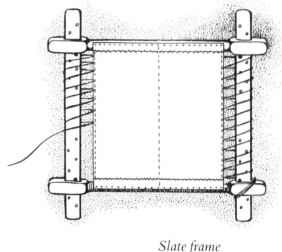

Slate frame

Tambour frame

upon the size and weight of the fabric you are using. The illustration shows fabric being stretched on a slate frame; for smaller pieces of work a tambour frame is perfectly adequate. Any frame which is mounted on a stand is much easier to use than one held in the hand, because it leaves both hands free to manipulate the needle.

Needles

Use as fine a needle as you can, remembering that, except in special circumstances, the needle should not be so thick that it distorts the weave of the fabric, but should be thick enough for the thread to follow it smoothly without tugging. Ideally you should collect a variety of sizes of crewel (sharp point with a long eye) and tapestry (blunt point with a long eye) needles to ensure you always have available the most useful needle for the work in hand. Other needles may be added for special purposes as and when they are needed.

Scissors

You will need a good pair of small, sharp scissors. This is not an item for economy – buy the best you can afford, and keep them exclusively for embroidery. No designing with cut paper, nor making plastic templates, with these treasures, please.

Thimbles

Few people nowadays are taught to use a thimble. This is a great pity since for many types of needlework they are a necessity, and for all types they are an advantage, once you get used to wearing one. Be sure to get a thimble which fits you comfortably, and use it on the second finger of your working hand. A silver thimble is a lovely thing to have, and ceramic thimbles are pretty things to collect, but for use a steel thimble is probably best.

Threads

The variety of threads on the market grows daily. The beginner would probably be best advised to concentrate on stranded cotton and crewel or tapestry wool for the first attempts, but it will not be long before you want to graduate to more exciting options. There are few hard and fast rules about the use of threads, though traditionally embroiderers would use silk threads on silk; silk or wool on woollen fabrics; wool on canvas; and linen, cotton or silk on linen. The range of synthetic threads available should not be neglected. Gold work techniques, for instance, can now be practised much more economically than in the past with coloured aluminium threads, and with metallized plastics in thread or sheet form.

Similarly, over the past few years many fabrics have been added to the embroiderer's repertoire. A typical example is Bondaweb (called by other names in other countries), a double-sided adhesive film which makes appliqué simplicity itself, while 'vanishing muslins' provide a temporary base for machine-embroidered lace.

Sketch books

One often forgotten but vital item of equipment for the embroiderer is a small sketch book. Carry it with you always, to record the ideas you will surely forget by the time you get home, no matter how inspired you were originally. Be sure to note when and where you find the inspiration, as well as details of colour! A counsel of perfection would be to file these sketches, together with newspaper and magazine cuttings, photographs, postcards from museums and other pieces of memorabilia, in transparent plastic envelopes in an indexed looseleaf file so that the sketch or photograph you want is always easy to find when required.

CHAPTER ONE

Prehistory

The Oxford dictionary defines history as 'the continuous methodical record of public events', from which we may assume that prehistory is that period of a people's culture which pre-dated any form of writing. Over the past two centuries the artefacts discovered and interpreted by archaeologists have told us a great deal about early humans who left no written records of their way of life. We are constantly awed and amazed at the massive constructions and the works of art that have survived for us to see, either because they are made of durable stone, like Stonehenge or the Menhirs in Brittany, or have been protected from the elements, as have the cave paintings in southern Europe.

Elk from Lascaux

On a holiday visit to Spain, many years ago, I was fortunate enough to visit the caves at Altamira. We were led first through well-lit, quite spacious caves until the roofs and walls closed in and the fixed lights became fewer. For the last part of the winding way we followed the torch of our guide until we came at length into a low 'room'. Here the original floor had been excavated around the perimeter, so we could stand and crane our necks as the guide shone her torch on the eerily lifelike animals which crowded the roof. Alternatively we could lie back on a thoughtfully placed mattress in the centre to study the figures more comfortably.

We had come in a group of twenty chattering tourists, hushed by the gloom for only the last few feet before entering the claustrophobic gallery in which the paintings had remained hidden for millennia. We could only experience a faint echo of what it must have felt like, those thousands of years ago, to crawl through the dark, carrying one's own taper, to see the figures when they were new. And what compulsion forced the artists to creep there in the darkness to make the record? We can only guess.

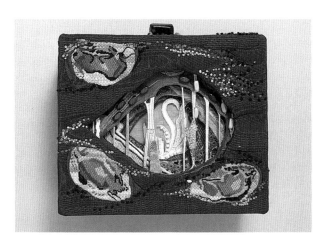

ABOVE *Nesting boxes, inspired by the cave paintings at Lascaux. Worked in a variety of techniques, these were designed and worked by Tryphena Orchard*

LEFT *Beaded necklace inspired by the colours of the cave paintings at Altamira. This was worked on a bead loom*

Obviously we can only guess at the culture and beliefs of these early people. It has been suggested that these paintings may have been offerings, either to ensure or to celebrate good hunting.

Offerings were made to propitiate all kinds of supernatural beings. The three-dimensional representations of women found in museums all over Europe may well have been votive offerings to a fertility deity. Other sources of design include pottery from prehistoric sites.

Female Images
a *Early Bronze Age idols from Mesopotamia, 3000BC*
b *Ivory statuette, the Venus de Lespugne*
c *Baked clay figure from Moravia*
d *Prehistoric carved limestone figure, now in the museum at Cagliari*

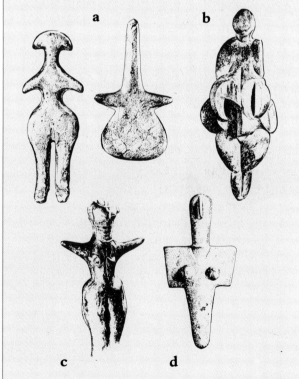

Prehistoric pottery
a *Egypt, 4000 BC, Pre-dynastic ware*
b *Earthenware vessels from Bosnia*
c *Urn found in West Prussia*
d *Earthenware vessel from North America*

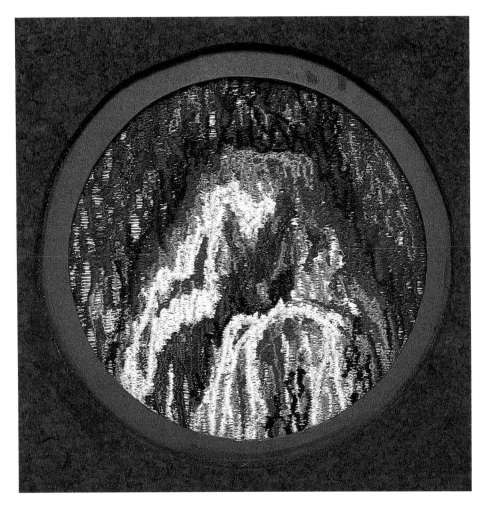

A design based on colours and shapes from the Cheddar Caves, worked in machine embroidery on evenweave linen. A piece of linen scrim was mounted in a tambour frame. The presser foot was removed from the machine and the feed mechanism dropped. The drawing was then worked by moving the frame under the swing needle, gathering the scrim so that a contrasting background could show through when mounted, and building up the abstract shapes of the rock formation

Although caves in the British Isles have yielded no works of art, there is no doubt that those in the Cheddar Gorge in Somerset were inhabited by some of the earliest Britons. Bathed in modern electric light for the benefit of tourists, the colours are reminiscent of the hues used in the Altamira and Lascaux cave paintings, and set off a train of ideas which resulted in the study in machine embroidery above.

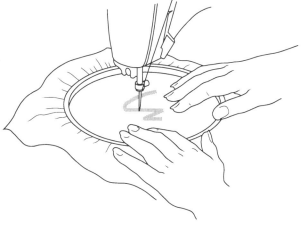

The most familiar prehistoric relic in England – possibly the most familiar in the whole of Europe, too – is the massive stone monument at Stonehenge in Wiltshire. An evocation in tent stitch of that lonely place could make an attractive memento of a visit.

Stonehenge in winter, based on a Second World War photograph by Bill Brandt. The panel is mainly in tent stitch worked horizontally, with a border worked in diagonal stitch

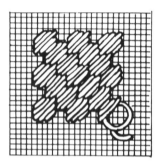

CHAPTER TWO

Ancient Mesopotamia

The Middle Eastern civilizations which depended upon the fertility of the lands watered by the Tigris and Euphrates rivers (known to us today as Iraq) arose about five thousand years ago, when the Sumerians came down from the north to settle around the head of the Persian Gulf. Archaeology has shown that these invaders adapted much of the technology of the people already living there and established small, walled cities, the chief of which was Ur. Their homes and temples were made of clay, and their inscriptions, the earliest form of record we know, were impressed upon wet clay tablets with small wedges of wood and then left to harden, or were fired for greater permanence.

King Darius hunting lions

Since there were no natural boundaries to protect the fertile land between the rivers, the history of the region consists of a long series of bloody wars and invasions. The Babylonians, Assyrians and Persians each took control in their turn as fortunes ebbed and flowed, their empires sometimes spreading as far as the Mediterranean, sometimes broken into many separate states, warring against each other.

One of the most peaceful and prosperous periods enjoyed by the people near the Gulf was during the reign of Hammurabi of Babylon (1792–1750 BC). Many documents of the time have come down to us in translation, or have been rediscovered by archaeologists. One of the most important was Hammurabi's collection of laws, which give a clear picture of the society of the time. So firm a pattern did this code impress that, with minor changes, it persisted until the Persian conquest in 539 BC.

It was the conquest by Alexander of Macedon in 333 BC which effectively ended this era. Greek ideas, customs and art forms were imposed upon the region and remained in place until they were gradually blended with those of the Romans.

ABOVE *Detail from the Standard of Ur*

BELOW *A sphinx from the Ishtar Gate at Babylon*

Memories of these great civilizations were passed down to the modern world through the pages of the Bible and through the writings of Greek historians, but for centuries the sites of their great cities were all but forgotten. Then in the eighteenth century amateur archaeologists started excavating the eroded remains which dotted the desert, and in the nineteenth century a series of finds proved that the magnificence reported in the Bible was in no way exaggerated. Much of the material was removed and shipped to the Louvre in Paris and the British Museum in London, where it astounds visitors still.

Since the Babylonian and Assyrian empires disappeared over 2500 years ago, none of their textiles have survived. Our knowledge of their decoration rests mainly upon bas-reliefs and glazed tiles found in the excavated ruined palaces, but these provide a remarkably rich visual record. It seems obvious from these statues and reliefs that embroidery was employed extensively in the decoration of garments, though the methods used are by no means clear.

A favourite motif was the flower in a circle: three versions from ancient Mesopotamia

BELOW RIGHT *Detail of a glazed tile from Nimrud, depicting Ashurnasirpal II taking a cup of wine*

Guilloche adapted as a pattern for corded quilting

Just how the simple pattern below was worked is open to question. Since it was part of the costume worn by a warrior it may possibly indicate armour made of plaques of metal sewn on to a fabric or leather base, or it could equally have been a quilted material to afford protection against blows.

TOP LEFT *Drawing of pattern on the 'shirt' of a soldier, interpreted* TOP RIGHT *in quilting* BOTTOM LEFT *in canvaswork* BOTTOM RIGHT *in machine appliqué*

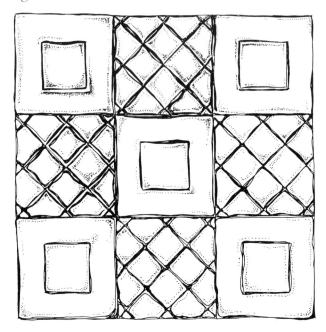

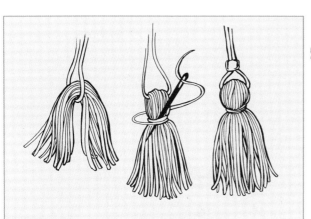

The method of making a simple tassel

From the wealth of sculptured portraits it would appear that a feature common to almost all ceremonial costume was the tassel. It appeared either at the end of a belt or sash, or as a trim on the bottom of a robe.

Tassels in colours found in Assyrian tiles

ABOVE *The demon Pazazu*
BELOW *Dragon from the Ishtar Gate at Babylon*

ABOVE *The hero of the famous Babylonian Epic of Gilgamesh subduing a lion*

The Babylonians believed that life was complicated by demons who even interfered with the dictates of the gods. It is interesting that one of the first delineations of the winged 'human' form occurs in Babylonian art – the demon Pazazu. It is a happy thought that Babylonian demons were unusually unsuspecting and of extremely low intelligence, so could easily be tricked and outwitted. Besides the dragons and other mythical animals, the reliefs show many naturalistic renditions of animals.

In a sun-baked land any greenery was treasured – witness the fame of the hanging gardens of Babylon. The representations of trees and rushes on the bas-reliefs at Nimrud would translate easily into embroidery.

It is quite impossible in one short chapter to give more than the briefest outline of a series of civilizations that lasted for 2500 years. If you find this region and this period of history interesting, do visit museums and libraries to conduct your own research: it is a very rich field.

Borders and patterns from Babylon and Assyria

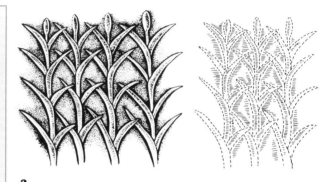

a

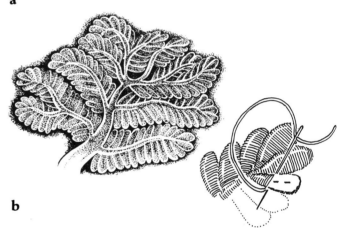

b

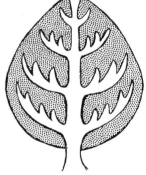

c

Bas-reliefs from Nimrud, showing how they might work as
a *quilting*
b *in satin stitch, and*
c *in appliqué*

OPPOSITE *Assyrian panel of machine embroidery and hand stitchery combined with painting on fabric. Designed and worked by Valerie McWilliams*

CHAPTER THREE

The Land of Egypt

So far as can be established, the Egyptian civilization first emerged from the mists of antiquity about three thousand years BC, and lasted until the Roman era. Because it was cut off from the rest of the world by the Mediterranean and by the deserts on either side of the Nile, Egypt suffered relatively little from the frequent invasions which introduced new ideas to other civilizations. As a result, styles of decoration continued with little major change until finally supplanted by the innovations of the Greeks and Romans.

Nomads, from the tomb of Khnum-hotep

Panel inspired by ancient Egyptian motifs.
Designed and worked by Diana Dolman

Our knowledge of this civilization derives mainly from the massive statues and buildings which still survive, and from the wealth of grave goods preserved by the dry desert air. The Egyptian cult of the dead insisted that the deceased be accompanied by all the things necessary in the afterlife – or a representation thereof.

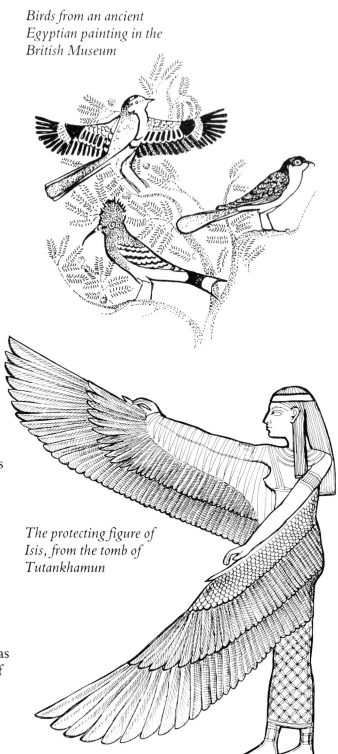

Birds from an ancient Egyptian painting in the British Museum

Slave bearing an offering

The protecting figure of Isis, from the tomb of Tutankhamun

We tend to think of Egyptian representations of the human form as stilted, particularly since they are shown, somewhat awkwardly to Western eyes, in profile. This technique was certainly true of most of the figures incised and painted on the walls of tombs, and painted on papyrus, but Egyptian artists were capable of very realistic painting too, especially of birds and animals.

Sculpture in the round was often quite realistic, though detail tended to be simplified. The gold bas-relief of the goddess Isis (right) has a relaxed feel, but retains the profile drawing of the feet. Note also the unusual approach to the winged figure, with the wings attached to the arms, not growing separately from the shoulders. A much more logical approach, anatomically, than most!

Many of the tombs of the kings of Egypt had fallen prey to grave robbers long before the archaeologists found them, but a few survived intact. The most famous is the tomb of Tutankhamun, who lived from 1343 to 1325 BC. Although his grave was broken into some time before 1133 BC, the robbers had been interrupted and the seals replaced. When the tomb was finally opened in 1922 the contents were complete, but considerably disturbed. The rich store of goods is now preserved in a Cairo museum, from which selections are sometimes loaned to other museums.

One recurring motif in Egyptian art is the imperial cobra, surmounted by the disc of the sun. On the back of a chair in the tomb this forms the top border of the decoration, with glass pieces inset in gold.

TOP LEFT *The repeated Cobra motif* TOP RIGHT *Chart for cross stitch or tent stitch* BOTTOM LEFT *The motif worked in cross stitch* BOTTOM RIGHT *The motif worked in satin stitch*

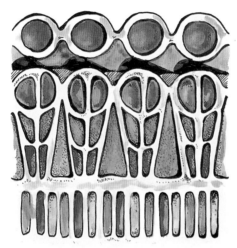

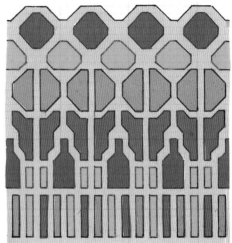

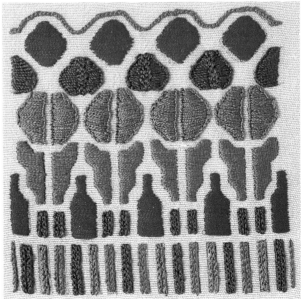

Pharaoh in ceremonial attire

Little Egyptian embroidery has been found in tombs, although the paintings and jewelled work indicate that it must have been used quite extensively. Whether the robes of the nomads (p. 22) were decorated with woven patterns or embroidered is impossible to tell.

Evidence from the Egyptian tombs would suggest that royalty dressed mainly in very finely woven linen, often delicately pleated, with decoration consisting chiefly of heavy jewellery in gold, precious stones and faience.

The Egyptians evolved a style of writing based on pictographs. When the Greeks and then the Romans took over the keeping of records in Egypt, the meaning behind these decorative symbols was lost until it was rediscovered in the nineteenth century. Then the so-called Rosetta Stone, which had a decree inscribed in Greek, in Egyptian hieroglyphs and Egyptian demotic (written) symbols, provided the key.

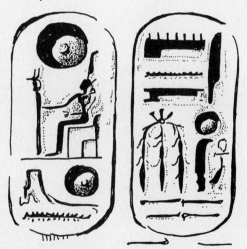

Cartouche showing the name of Rameses (1296–1294 BC)

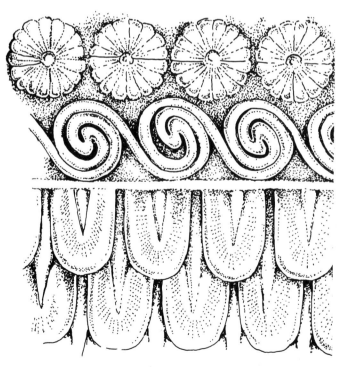

Embossed designs from Tutankhamun's chariot

The papyrus plant which fringed the Nile and provided the raw material for Egyptian records was a major source of design, although the lotus comes a close second. Border and spot designs are illustrated, although overall designs are also very common.

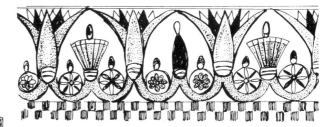

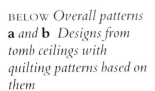

BELOW *Overall patterns* **a** *and* **b** *Designs from tomb ceilings with quilting patterns based on them* **c** *Mummy case in the Louvre* **d** *Dress of a figure in a royal tomb, indicating scales of armour*

ABOVE AND RIGHT *Designs based on the papyrus plant*

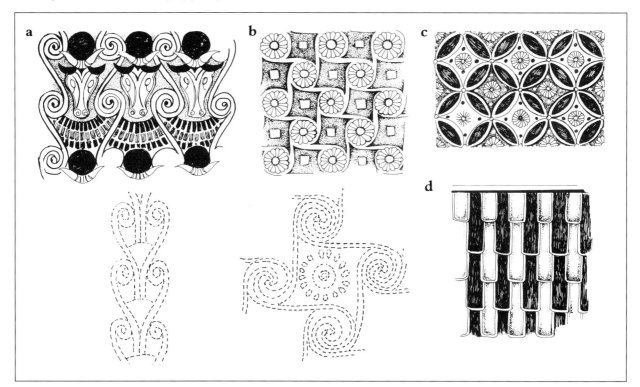

a

b

c

d

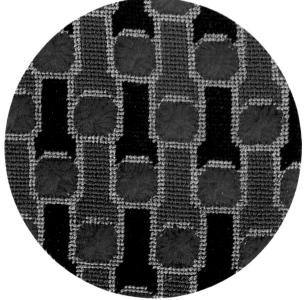

ABOVE *Feather design from Tutankhamun's coffin case with an interpretation in canvaswork. The methods used to indicate feathers in Egyptian gold and faience work, as shown in this elaborate hawk pendant* RIGHT, *could easily be translated into reverse appliqué or used as a repeat motif in cutwork or quilting*

28

CHAPTER FOUR

Ancient Greece

To the modern tourist, ancient Greece means weathered creamy marble temples baking under a burning sun against a cobalt sky. It is easy to imagine that the buildings were glowing white when they were new, but evidence confounds this impression as the Greeks decorated everything they could with exuberant colour, picked out with gold. The internal walls of their homes were covered with painted murals, both naturalistic and purely decorative, while their floors were inlaid with mosaics in the liveliest of patterns. There was colour everywhere.

Dancing girls from an Athenian cup

Greek civilization, unlike that of either Assyria or Egypt, was not bound by the strictures of religious symbolism. Its art could therefore be much freer and develop according to the imagination and skill of the artist. From the earliest times the works of art which have come down to us display a freedom and a vigour which we still find very attractive.

The most familiar specimens of Greek design are found on the black and terracotta pottery displayed in museums all over the world. These are frequently decorated with scenes depicting stories from Greek mythology, combined with borders of stylized flowers.

ABOVE RIGHT *Greek vase from the British Museum*

ABOVE LEFT *A pebble mosaic floor from Ai Khanum, a city founded in Mesopotamia in the wake of Alexander and peopled with Greek settlers*

ABOVE AND LEFT *Stylized Greek floral patterns*

The Greek civilization forms the basis of our own. We owe to it many concepts such as comedy and tragedy in literature, and architectural forms which are still in use today.

If you visit a museum which houses artefacts from Athens and Corinth, or from any of the Greek city states scattered around the Aegean shore, the only rich colour you are likely to see will be the range of hot browns found in Greek pottery. The graceful shapes of the vessels are satisfying in themselves, but the wealth of pattern found upon them could keep an embroiderer occupied for years: the geometric borders beg to be reproduced in cross stitch on linen, or in wool on canvas, whilst the floral and serpentine patterns lend themselves to interpretation by other techniques.

Mask of Tragedy

Mask of Comedy

An assortment of Greek patterns suitable for cross stitch borders

Athens was the principal city state of the Greek civilization. The symbol both of Athens and of Athena, the goddess of wisdom, was the owl.

It would seem from the sculpture of the period that the costume worn in classical Greece was a graceful drapery in white linen. However, some murals suggest the use of solid colours with woven or embroidered bands of decoration.

The Greeks obviously did not share the earlier belief in winged human figures – their inherent pragmatism gives us, instead, the tragic story of Icarus whose wings were provided by his father, Daedalus. The nearest they came to the older legends was the winged horse, Pegasus.

Although the Greeks achieved standards in painting, sculpture and architecture which were unsurpassed until the Renaissance, our most readily accessible source of Greek design is the store of pottery housed in our museums. I am particularly fond of the stylized warriors from such sources. On p.34, I try to convey something of the atmosphere of these images.

ABOVE *Two Athenian coins from the fifth century BC showing the owl, symbol of the goddess Athena, with* LEFT *an interpretation in machine embroidery*

BELOW *Horses from Greek vases*

ABOVE *Figure from the Temple of Zeus at Olympia, dated approximately 460 BC*

ABOVE *Circular bosses from Greek and Macedonian sources, with quilting pattern*

LEFT *Quilting patterns from Hellenic mosaic floors, suitable for either corded or English quilting*

RIGHT *Panel based on Greek warriors. The distant figure is worked in blackwork, while his attacker in the foreground is made up of layers of nylon gauze fused to the linen with Bondaweb and then anchored with surface stitchery. Touches of gold plastic and metallic thread complete the composition*

ABOVE *Helmet of the great Athenian general Miltiades*

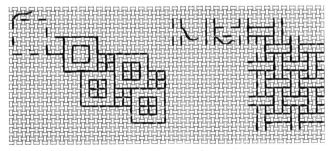

Two of the blackwork patterns used on the panel

The Greek world was eventually absorbed into the Roman sphere, but Greek art persisted, being admired and emulated by the Romans. It is therefore very difficult to draw an exact line between Greek and Roman design, and elements from both cultures are sometimes blended in a single piece of decoration.

CHAPTER FIVE

Rome

Whilst Alexander was conquering most of the known world, a small city state in central Italy began to expand its influence, warring with and eventually conquering its neighbours. By 270 BC Rome had assimilated the Etruscans and had subdued the Greek city states on the mainland of Italy and in Sicily.

Over the next five centuries Roman influence spread into North Africa, and westwards along the African shore of the Mediterranean towards Spain. Eastwards the Romans took over, piece by piece, most of what had been Alexander's empire, though they never penetrated so far into Asia as Alexander's influence had done.

ABOVE *From a mosaic floor, Fishbourne Palace, Chichester*
BELOW *Quilting pattern based on the border which encircles the cherub on a dolphin*

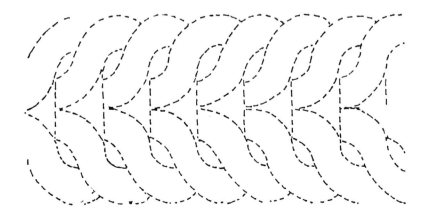

LEFT *Example of a Pompeian frieze, worked in silk using satin stitch, buttonhole stitch and French knots*
BELOW *Motif from the frieze with some of the stitches used*

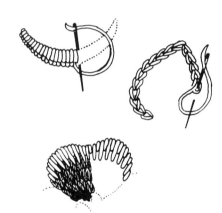

Unlike the Greeks, the Romans tended not to be innovators; their outstanding achievement was the amalgamation of the ideas of others into their own civilization. They borrowed and adapted the styles they admired, particularly from the Etruscans and the Greeks.

Their own contribution was the institution of order over a vast region, extending from Scotland to Africa and from Spain to the Middle East. Their rule was based on Roman law and sustained by a magnificent communications system and a disciplined professional army. Cities founded as outposts of Empire still bear the imprint of the orderly street plans they laid down, and modern highways follow the straight line of Roman roads. There also still exists an astonishing number of buildings which have been in continuous use for two thousand years.

The wealthier Romans enjoyed a standard of comfort not encountered again in Europe until the end of the nineteenth century. Pipes from the hills above Rome provided them with clean water and enabled them to build sewage systems; roads were paved and maintained; and, especially in cooler provinces, central heating was effected by underfloor hypocausts. It has been suggested that, without hypocausts, the Roman Empire would never have spread northwards.

Floors in public buildings and in the houses of the rich were paved with mosaic tiles, some geometric, others pictorial. These were more permanent, and more easily cleaned, than our carpets! Walls were adorned with bas-relief carvings, or with murals painted in fresco (water colours on fresh plaster).

Hundreds of years of wear and tear, war and natural disasters should have meant that we had little evidence of how splendidly the Romans lived. However, due to the eruption of Vesuvius in AD 79 it is possible for us to examine pristine examples of Roman art, protected from the ravages of time by volcanic ash until excavation of Pompeii and Herculaneum started in the eighteenth century.

Roman pattern seems quite familiar to us today, since it has served as a model for much of European design since the Renaissance. The Romans used the alphabet we inherited from them, and their lettering is still an inspiration to us. Vast numbers of examples have survived, from ceremonial inscriptions on monuments to graffiti scribbled on the walls of Pompeii.

VOLVSENA   EQVO

ABCDEFGHIJKLM
NOPQRSTUV
WXYZ
OPTIMO
AVGVRINA

Lettering from a Roman inscription in the Ducal Palace at Urbino, with (centre) a modern version of Roman lettering

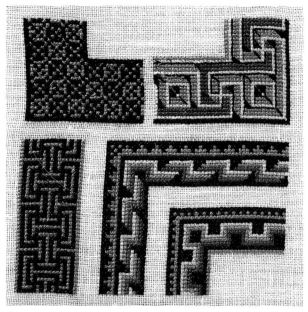

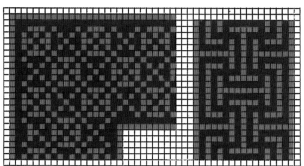

Cross stitch patterns from Roman floors with charts for two of them

Floor from Chedworth Villa in Gloucestershire

Two patterns from Roman architecture, with an indication of how they could be adapted for whitework embroidery

The surrounding patterns would be worked in padded satin stitch, the centres in pulled fabric stitches

The Empire persisted until the sack of Rome by invading tribesmen from eastern Europe in the fifth century AD. In an impoverished Italy, much of the civilization that the Empire had enjoyed was lost for nearly a thousand years. Only in a few Roman churches, and in the Eastern Empire that had been set up in Byzantium (modern Istanbul), was any trace preserved. Wild animals roamed in the Forum, and nothing but a memory remained of the glory that was Rome.

ABOVE *Elaborate Romano-Hellenic floor from Paphos in Cyprus, with a simplification for quilting and the method of working Italian quilting*

38

Design for cross stitch for a dove, based on a mosaic of drinking doves from excavations at the Villa Adriana at Tivoli

Patchwork quilt based on Roman floors. Designed and worked by Daphne Easterbrook

CHAPTER SIX

Byzantium

By the fourth century AD the Roman Empire had been declining for generations, as it became too large to govern efficiently. When Constantine became Emperor he decided that it would be logical to govern the Empire from a more convenient geographical point than Rome; he chose the small Greek settlement of Byzantium, at the point where Asia and Europe meet, to be his new capital. The name was officially changed to Constantinople, although for a long time it was better known as Nova Roma.

Although at the beginning almost the entire ruling class of the new city were Romans, with Latin remaining the official language, by the time the Western and Eastern parts of the Roman Empire separated, a hundred years later, Greek had replaced Latin. The Eastern Empire became known as Byzantium.

Despite persecution, Christianity had been gaining hold in Rome. By the time Constantine found it politic to make it the official religion, most Romans had already been converted. In Rome Christianity had been a democratically based religion, with elected leaders, but when Constantine settled in Constantinople he merged the posts of Head of Church and Head of State. This, and the emphasis on mysticism introduced by the Greeks and Syrians, eventually made the Eastern Church quite distinct from the Church of Rome.

Emperor Constantine, from an ivory reliquary made to house a fragment of the true cross, eleventh century

Floor patterns from the Basilica of St Mark in Venice and SS Maria and Donato in Murano

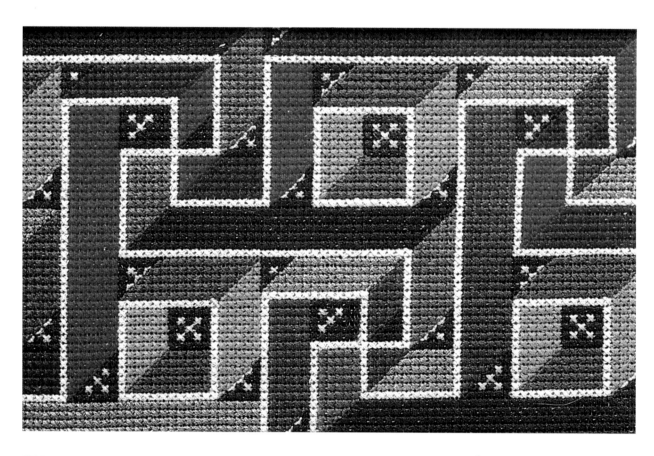

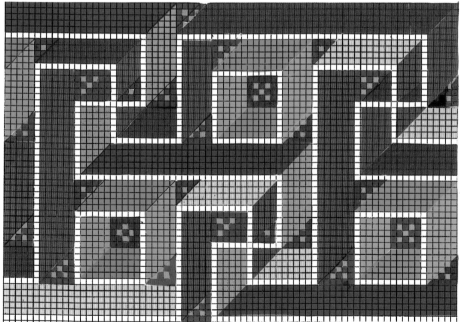

Book cover in cross stitch, based on mosaics in an archway in the Mausoleum of Galla Placidia in Ravenna, with chart for the cover. Half cross stitch allows one to achieve an effective diagonal

Shortly after the split, Italy was over-run by the Goths and in 402 the government hurriedly moved to Ravenna, in the safety of the marshes at the head of the Adriatic. Rome was left to be captured and looted. In 476 Ravenna too was taken, and the Western Roman Empire ceased to exist. When the Gothic conquerors of Ravenna embraced Christianity it was to the East they looked, not to Rome.

At its greatest extent, in the sixth century AD, the Byzantine Empire spread from Malaga in southern Spain to Trebizond on the Black Sea and as far south as the Red Sea, taking in both Antioch and Jerusalem. Untouched by the ravages of conquest which reduced the Western Empire to barbarism, throughout the Dark Ages Byzantium preserved the history and art of Greece and Rome. Under the Emperor Justinian there was a great flowering of Byzantine art. Though strict Church leaders later banned all representations of the human figure for a hundred years, the lifting of this ban triggered a second golden age.

By the end of the ninth century the Empire was beginning to fall apart. It became necessary to grant independent status to the Russians and

Patchwork cushions based upon Venetian floors, with diagrams of templates

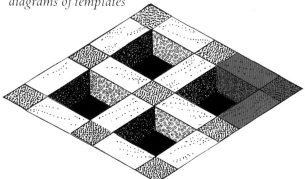

43

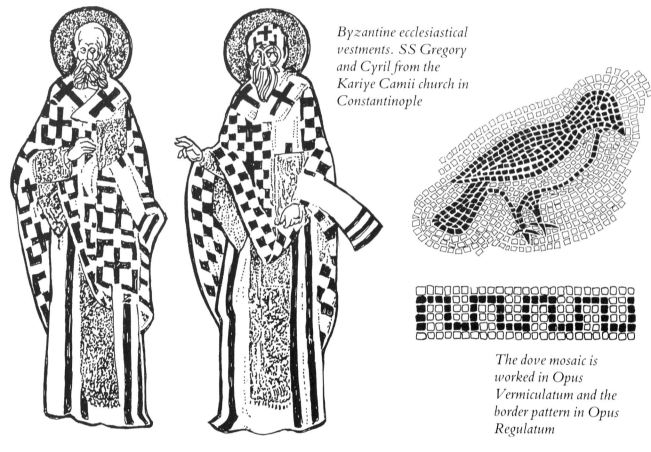

Byzantine ecclesiastical vestments. SS Gregory and Cyril from the Kariye Camii church in Constantinople

The dove mosaic is worked in Opus Vermiculatum and the border pattern in Opus Regulatum

the Serbs. The Spanish and North African colonies had been lost to invaders, and even Jerusalem was over-run by the followers of Mohammed.

Constantinople was sacked in 1204 by Crusaders who could not resist its wealth when pausing there, supposedly bent on recovering Jerusalem from the Infidel! They were not persuaded to leave for fifty years. Finally, in 1453 the city was conquered by the Ottoman Turks, and the Byzantine Empire ceased to exist.

The most magnificent relics of the Byzantine Empire to be found in Europe are the *smalti* (opaque glass) mosaics in Ravenna and Venice. Although most of the mosaics are worked in Opus Vermiculatum (where the lines of the mosaics follow, roughly, the outline of the figure), some are in Opus Regulatum; this technique can easily be translated into cross

stitch, especially if half cross stitch is used.

The figurative mosaics from Ravenna and Venice are as rich in colour as they were the day they were first made. Most backgrounds are gold, set irregularly so that the *smalti* catch the light and make the backgrounds appear iridescent.

The Venetian lagoon yields a wealth of mosaic mural decoration, particularly in the Cathedral on the island of Torcello. One of the richest Byzantine legacies is found on the floors of the older churches in Venice itself, particularly St Mark's. While some of the patterns are laid in Opus Vermiculatum, most are in Opus Sectile, where geometrical shapes of stone are cut and bedded in mastic to make marvellous patchwork patterns. Similar floors can be found in churches and public buildings all around the shores of the Aegean Sea.

The Byzantine style spread, with the Eastern version of Christianity, throughout the Slav countries. It is preserved today in the liturgy and vestments of the Greek and Russian Orthodox Churches.

During the whole of its existence the Empire traded with Asia, importing silks and precious stones from China and India. The sumptuous velvets and brocades which survive from the Byzantine court reflect this trade with the East. Other source materials for Byzantine design are to be found in the exquisite ivory carvings of the period such as that of the Emperor Constantine on p.41, and in icons – stylized religious images painted on wooden panels and often set with precious stones.

Two examples of Byzantine textile designs. There is another example on page 40

Icon in gold, appliqué and beadwork, based on Byzantine examples. The face is worked in tent stitch using a very fine silk thread on silk gauze

CHAPTER SEVEN

Celtic Art

Celtic ornament, which evolved from Iron Age decoration in northern Europe, particularly in Britain, is generally divided into two phases – the pre-Christian era, from about 250 BC to AD 600, and the period which followed the introduction of Christianity and reached its fullest flowering in the eleventh and twelfth centuries. The earlier period is nowadays represented chiefly by metalwork on military equipment for man and horse, recovered from burial mounds and the sites of battles. The craftsmen used divergent spirals and elliptical curves for their designs, filling the backgrounds with frets, interlaced work and diaper patterns. These motifs were further developed after the craftsmen were converted to Christianity, when these characteristic designs were used in religious monuments and manuscripts. Some exquisitely patterned and enamelled jewellery has also survived from this period.

Part of a border from the Lindisfarne Gospels

RIGHT *Interlaced patterns from Celtic sources, with adaptations for quilting*

ABOVE *Further quilting patterns from Celtic designs*

Some of the best examples of Celtic design available to us are found on the stone monuments which abound in Britain, particularly in those areas where Celtic influence persists to the present day – Scotland, Wales and Ireland. Further treasures exist in the beautifully illuminated manuscripts from the period, such as the Book of Kells and the Lindisfarne Gospels, to be found in major museums in the British Isles.

Celtic lettering is another fascinating source of inspiration. The lower case letters use a simple uncial style, most of the decoration being reserved for the capital initials. These can be quite simple, as in the example illustrated below, or wildly elaborate, incorporating interlacing human, animal and mythical figures.

There is an amazing wealth of material to work from in Celtic design. On p.50 is a collection of spot motifs which could be used for quilting, goldwork or surface stitchery of various types.

The word 'PEACE' embroidered in silk and embellished with paint

The Rossie Priory Stone

Celtic lettering

ABOVE *Fret designs from Celtic art, showing adaptations for quilting patterns, cross stitch and double running stitch*

LEFT *Method of working double running stitch*

Although they could be interpreted easily enough in surface stitchery, fret patterns cannot be translated directly into counted thread embroidery as they are worked on a 60° diagonal which does not coincide with the grid of woven fabric. By changing the design to incorporate right-angles the problem is eliminated, and they can then be worked quite normally in double running and cross stitch.

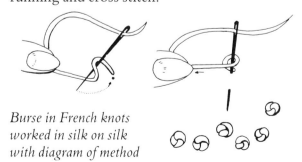

Burse in French knots worked in silk on silk with diagram of method

Spot motifs from various sites

*Part of a border from the
Lindisfarne Gospels*

One particular embroidery technique of the period was that displayed on the so-called Bayeux Tapestry (really an embroidery rather than a tapestry). Some years ago I worked a section as a sampler in order to teach myself how to do it. The horse on the panel shown on p. 51, inspired by the Rossie Priory Stone, was also worked in the Bayeux couching technique.

Horse from the Bayeux Tapestry, worked as a sampler

I drew the horse in the appropriate size and then transferred my drawing on to a coarse linen fabric stretched on a frame. I anchored green woollen threads by taking small back stitches at the centre top of the cloak area and then laying them vertically, up and down, across the area of the cloak. (It is not necessary to carry threads behind the fabric if a space is left between the strands to be filled in on a return journey.)

I then anchored another thread of the same colour at the centre of one side of the cloak and laid it across at right-angles to the first layer, taking it down at the edge of the cloak and bringing it up again about ⅜in (10mm) in to catch (couch) the thread in place, continuing across the work at regular intervals. I laid a second thread at a suitable interval below, and again caught it down. Such couching stitches must not lie directly above each other as this causes a split to open up, exposing the fabric beneath. Where the pattern allows, a brick pattern works best. I completed the cloak by working from the centre up.

All solid areas were worked in the same fashion. In the Bayeux Tapestry faces were worked in stem stitch, as were reins, horses' tails and other details. Stem stitch also outlined the areas of laid work.

ABOVE LEFT *Drawing of horse to be transferred to fabric* ABOVE RIGHT *Method of working* BELOW *Panel from the Rossie Priory stone; the mount is worked in cross stitch and double running stitch*

CHAPTER EIGHT

Islamic Art

When the followers of Mohammed carried the Islamic faith eastwards to Syria and Persia, and westwards along the North African shore to Spain, they made use at first of the buildings and decorative arts they found among the peoples they subdued. The Islamic conquerors turned existing churches and temples into mosques and retained the services of the local craftsmen to embellish them, often keeping the major part of the original decorations. It took several centuries before characteristic art forms evolved in the various regions which had become Muslim, but the tenets of the religion and the constant interchange of ideas among the followers of Islam ensured a certain cohesiveness of design everywhere the new religion spread.

Earthenware wall tiles, Syrian, 1425, Victoria and Albert Museum

Most easily accessible to Europeans are the designs still used in North Africa. They can be found in the palaces and other buildings still standing in Granada and Seville, in what was once Moorish Spain.

The Arabic culture which prevailed in North Africa and Spain was intrigued by mathematical problems. The tile patterns on p.54, easily translatable into patchwork, illustrate this interest.

Designs from North African ceramic tiles

Moorish patterns from Granada in Spain

ABOVE *Arabic tile patterns, with* BELOW *patchwork based on Arabic designs*

OPPOSITE *Designs from the Alhambra, including an interpretation as a patched and quilted wall hanging or cot quilt*

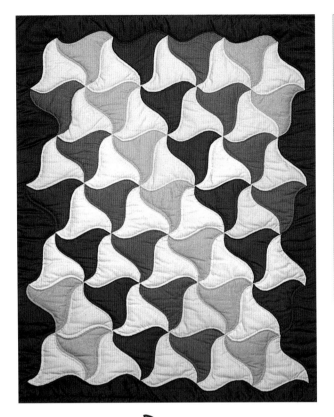

Although in some Islamic cultures the use of the human figure was frowned upon, if not actually forbidden, it continued to be used in Persia (Iran) until recent times, and delicate Persian miniatures were much treasured. In other parts of the Muslim world, although the human figure was outlawed, animal forms, flowers and foliage became major sources of design.

The Islamic faith is now spread all across the globe, apart from the Americas, where it is only meagrely represented. It is easy to forget how much Western civilization has owed to Islamic culture over the centuries; for instance, the numerals we use come directly from Arabia, as does the algebraic system.

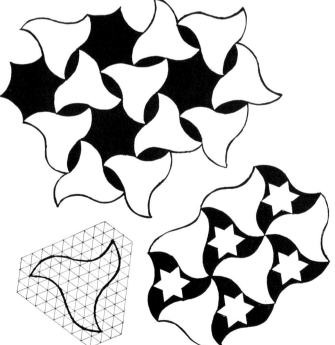

Persian dish, twelfth century

*Persian faience plate,
fourteenth century*

ABOVE *Carved glass
bottle with silhouette of
running hare, Persian,
tenth century*

LEFT *Panel based on
flowers from Persian
carpets, in satin stitch,
buttonhole stitch, French
knots and spider webs*

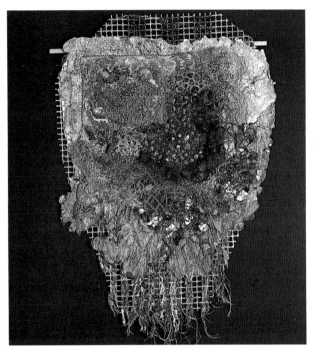

Wall decoration in the palace of Ismail Bey,
fourteenth century

Detail of
fourteenth-century fabric

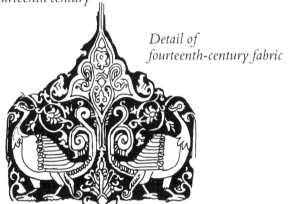

ABOVE *Panel based on
the Alhambra Vase in
the Museo del Arte,
Granada; designed and
worked by Sandra
Kedzlie. This huge
lustre vase, standing
about 4 feet (122cm)
high, was produced about
the time of Columbus,
using techniques which
originated in Persia but
were perfected in Malaga
in the tenth century. The
panel is worked mostly in
machine embroidery,
using vanishing fabrics
and scrim, with dyed
threads and painted
fabrics*
RIGHT *experimentation
and source material for
the panel*

CHAPTER NINE

Medieval Europe

The medieval period in Europe, often known as the Middle Ages, covers much of the thousand years between the culture of antiquity and the Renaissance. It was a period of turmoil and almost constant war, with the Roman Empire recalled as the golden age in the past; its recreation in the 'Holy Roman Empire' was seen as the goal to strive for.

Pockets of recognizable civilization survived the southward surge of the Germanic invaders, the threat of the Turks from the east and the Moors from Africa. These were nurtured chiefly by the Roman Church, which kept alive a conservative, theology-based education. For centuries few people learned to read other than those dedicated to a monastic life, and Latin remained the language of the Church. In an increasingly polyglot Europe this universal tongue was very useful, but it meant that the common people were excluded from any possibility of gaining power and knowledge except through the Church.

One of the many medieval alphabets

The powerful men who waged wars protected themselves so completely with heavy armour that it became necessary to find some method of identifying each other in battle. Thus was heraldry born; in time it became a 'science', with a language of its own.

From a painting by Simone Martini, Siena, about 1328. Trappings of horse and rider appear to be patchwork plus embroidery

Encaustic floor tiles (of contrasting colours of clay), thirteenth and fourteenth centuries

passant

statant

sejant

couchant

dormant

passant regardant

sejant erect

rampant guardant

queue fourche

double headed

A selection of heraldic lions

The physical sciences, so much cherished in Islamic countries, were almost totally neglected in Europe, and the spirit of scepticism was discouraged. Superstition was everywhere, whether it was evidenced in the tenacity of pagan, pre-Christian belief such as the Green Man legends, or in the thousands who were convinced that the rigours of pilgrimage to holy places would earn them a smooth road to Paradise when they died.

In the Green Man panel illustrated, the face of the green man was first sculpted in plasticine, then covered with papier mâché. When this was dry, a stretch velvet material was laid over the papier mâché and the details quilted through all layers. Before fixing to the panel the spaces were stuffed with wadding so that any pressure would not result in fractures. The embroidery was then completed using pulled fabric techniques, surface stitchery and canvas stitches. Some of the leaves were constructed separately with layers of felt or satin, and stitched to the base material. Threads used varied from fine silk for the pulled work to knitting wools and chenille for the bolder stitches.

With travel limited to horseback for the wealthy, and by foot to any others determined to seek fresh horizons, it is not surprising that the known world was centred on the Mediterranean and that all manner of strange tales abounded, of men and animals beyond the fringes of knowledge. Many descriptions of fantastic creatures were accepted as true, and incorporated into the illuminated manuscripts so lovingly produced in religious houses and translated into heraldry. Other animals, real enough, were drawn from second- or third-hand descriptions and would hardly be recognizable when compared with the reality.

TOP *Green Man panel, based on the studies* LEFT *showing a Green Man from Radnor church, Powys, a horned god from Belvoir Castle, Leicestershire and a carved border from Winchester Cathedral*

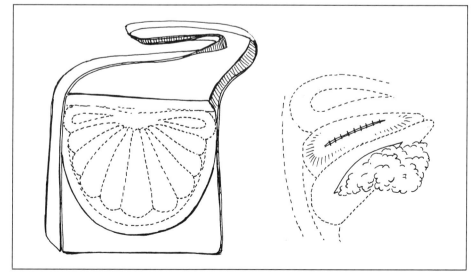

Mythical animals
ABOVE *phoenix*
LEFT *cockatrice*

Pilgrims, from the Cathedral of St Lazare at Autun in France. The pouches of the pilgrims could easily be translated for modern use by employing Trapunto quilting (reverse side shown here)

RIGHT *Archvolt of a doorway, Peterborough Cathedral* FAR RIGHT *arches from Rochester Cathedral, Kent*

Stained glass panel, 'Pisces' – a detail from the Zodiac window at Chartres

Emulating stained glass ABOVE *The coloured fabrics are butted together, the join covered with a bias rouleau and stitched in place.* BELOW *The butted coloured fabrics are covered with one piece of dark cloth, the surplus cut away and turnings hemmed to reveal the pattern*

In spite of the instability of life at these times, and because of the faith which was all that so many people had to cling to, the building of great churches flourished. The crafts allied to this endeavour reached a very high standard of excellence. The enamels and gold work of the period continue to astound us, and medieval stained glass is treasured wherever it is still to be found. In England the craft of embroidery reached such a peak that Church embroidery – known as Opus Anglicanum – was ordered by the Popes in Rome, or given to them as presents. A considerable quantity of this beautiful work survives today.

The winged human form, which the Greeks had scorned, reappeared in many variations during this period. The multi-winged seraph was the most extreme example.

RIGHT *Enamelled seraph from Cologne, about 1180*

FAR RIGHT *The Hastings Brass in Elsing church, Norfolk, about 1348*

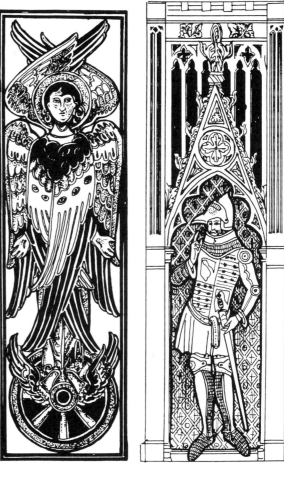

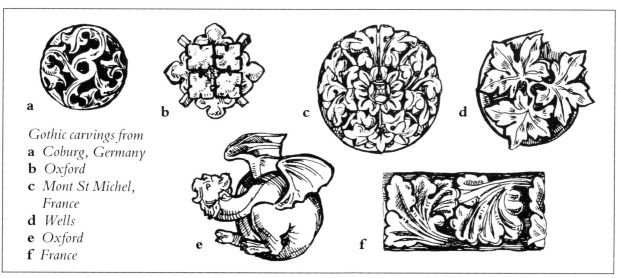

Gothic carvings from
a *Coburg, Germany*
b *Oxford*
c *Mont St Michel, France*
d *Wells*
e *Oxford*
f *France*

CHAPTER TEN

The Renaissance

The Renaissance or revival of learning marks the beginning of modern Europe. It did not happen all at once, but emerged slowly from the medieval era, heralded by writers such as Dante in Italy and Chaucer in England, and by painters such as Giotto and Masaccio in Italy. The Renaissance was marked by a new outburst of individualism, a new freedom of thought and action, and an avid speculation concerning this world and the next.

Although politically disunited, and frequently in a state of upheaval, Italy was the fertile soil in which the Renaissance was rooted. Many of the Italian states possessed the standard of wellbeing necessary for cultural development, and their inhabitants lived amongst the remnants of the Roman Empire, as well as having trading connections with Constantinople and the East.

A detail from the Ghiberti Gate, Florence

The medieval world had produced the theology-based specialist. The Renaissance honoured the man of multiple talents, of which Leonardo da Vinci is the example that springs immediately to mind.

Although the medieval world had never entirely lost touch with classical literature, many old manuscripts were now rediscovered and copied. Excavations in Roman ruins brought forth examples of Roman art to spur the painters and sculptors of the Renaissance.

The Humanist philosophies, which exalted man's own potential rather than God's achievements, now spread throughout Europe. They were particularly well received in places such as the Low Countries (modern Belgium and Holland), which were prosperous centres of trade. Since reform within the Church was proving slow and difficult, the new Humanism led to the schisms of the Reformation, the emergence of the Protestant Churches and the bitter religious divisions which followed.

The development of printing hastened the dissemination of these new ideas. Starting with the Bible, it helped to put knowledge into the hands of a much wider public than had previously been possible.

Example of Italian Renaissance lettering

One result of the proliferation of printed books was the circulation of the bestiaries of Conrad Gesner, first published in 1551, drawings from which were used as embroidery patterns. These were closely followed by embroidery pattern books, from which the alphabet shown here, designed for lacis (embroidered net), was taken.

Six letters from a lacis alphabet, with one method of working lacis

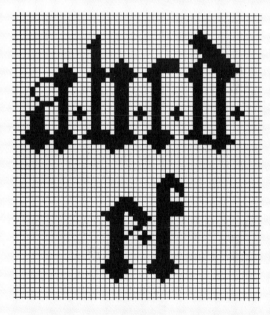

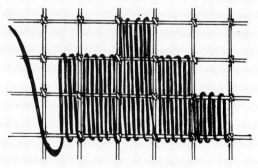

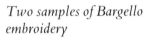

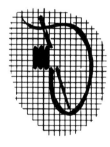

Two samples of Bargello embroidery

Three charts showing other patterns. The embroidery was worked in upright Gobelin stitch, as shown below. Alternatively it could be done in knitting stitch

A style of embroidery which appears to date from this period is Bargello or Hungarian point, also known as Florentine embroidery, which was popular in Italy in the fifteenth and sixteenth centuries. It was used on the upholstery of chairs, as a decorative covering for walls, and even for ecclesiastical vestments.

An interest in nature, already evidenced in the decoration of medieval manuscripts, now become even more pronounced. House furnishings were embellished with painted and carved renditions of the animals of the chase, and from exotic collections brought back by explorers, as well as with scenes from ordinary domestic life. Every possible flower and fruit from the Renaissance garden was also employed as decoration. These subjects were embroidered enthusiastically on to the clothing and soft furnishings of the era.

Renaissance ideas spread to most regions of Europe. In England they reached a peak in the sixteenth century, with the writings of Shakespeare and his contemporaries and the flowering of a society which appreciated the

Charts for fruit and a bird taken from Elizabethan slip designs, originally intended for painstaking application on to velvet

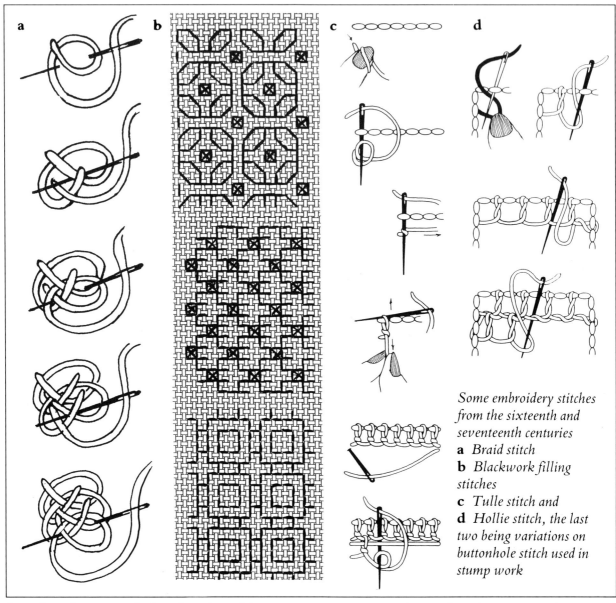

*Some embroidery stitches
from the sixteenth and
seventeenth centuries*
a *Braid stitch*
b *Blackwork filling
stitches*
c *Tulle stitch and*
d *Hollie stitch, the last
two being variations on
buttonhole stitch used in
stump work*

beauties of nature, echoing them in architecture, poetry, embroidery and many other fields of human endeavour. Although some fragments of embroidery from earlier eras have survived, this is the first period which provides a wealth of material for us to study.

Although records show that much embroidery was done by craft guilds in the cities, or in religious houses, much of the surviving work was done by wives, relatives and servants of landowners, who all lived in the great houses which a less warlike era allowed to be built and maintained over much of Europe.

Gloves were frequently presented as special gifts to a patron or a visiting dignitary. These were exchanged in such profusion that some have come down to us unworn, and can provide inspiration to the modern embroiderer.

*Portrait Doll of Queen Elizabeth I, designed and
worked by Angela Gibson*

BELOW LEFT *Drawing of an Elizabethan glove, and*
RIGHT *a gauntlet based on the idea of a Renaissance
glove, designed and worked by Dorothy Beckett*

CHAPTER ELEVEN

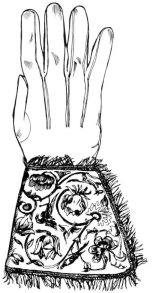

Pre-Columbian Mexico

In 1519, when Hernan Cortez landed with 533 men and 16 horses near what is now Vera Cruz in Mexico, he was looking for gold, and the first ambassadors from the Aztec ruler Montezuma brought him gifts which only served to whet his appetite. In spite of the small size of his 'army' he was able to stir some of the coastal tribes to revolt against the central government, and to play upon the superstitious belief of the emperor that the white-skinned, bearded Spaniards heralded the predicted return of the god Quetzalcoatl.

Despite one disastrous defeat, Cortez was able to subdue the vastly larger numbers of Aztecs. Smallpox, inadvertently introduced by the Spaniards to a population with no immunity to the disease, finished the task and within a very few years the whole of the Central American landmass was subject to the Spaniards.

Illustrations from a manuscript, showing funeral rites

Only a minority of the Spanish conquerors appreciated the society or the art of the Mexican people. Some gold ornaments were sent back to the Spanish court, and thus preserved, but most of the golden artefacts were melted down for ease of shipment. Revolted by the human sacrifice which was a part of the religion of the 'Indians', the Spaniards did their utmost to convert them to Christianity, often by means which were scarcely less barbaric than the practices they sought to suppress. Within a matter of decades the Indian tribes had become the down-trodden workforce of the land-hungry Spaniards, who wanted to found a new Spain in Central America.

RIGHT *Zapotec maize god from a clay urn. The feathered head-dress incorporates the face of a bat. Evidence of the Zapotec culture was found on the Pacific coast, in south-eastern Mexico*

ABOVE *Mayan hieroglyph from Palenque, Mexico. The writing of ancient America is as yet only partially deciphered*

RIGHT *Panel based on the Zapotec maize god and other similar figures*

Our knowledge of Pre–Columbian life in Mexico rests largely on a few dozen manuscripts recording the Aztec society so soon to be destroyed. These were illustrated by Aztec artists, with texts by Spanish priests, and were designed to explain his new subjects to the Spanish king. For many years they reposed in the archives in Madrid, until the reawakening of interest in the past sent scholars back to this invaluable source material. During this century these manuscripts have been supplemented by exhaustive archaeological investigations of cities which had been overwhelmed by jungle, many even before the arrival of the Spaniards.

Although the Pre–Columbian 'Indians' had a very exact calendar, and recorded events in stone by means of hieroglyphics, these have not yet been accurately deciphered. When this does happen we will understand a great deal more about the civilizations which came to an abrupt end at the beginning of the sixteenth century.

Many hundreds of malacates – spindle whorls like the one from the illustration in the Codex Vindobonensis – have survived. Their top surfaces were usually decorated with lustre slips and stamped, or had incised designs. The blank circle in the centre of the round shape of the

Woman spinning, from the manuscript known as the Codex Vindobonensis

design is the recess in which the spindle revolves. These simple, flat designs lend themselves readily to various forms of quilting, whether it be simple English quilting, or the much more elaborate version shown on p.73.

To work a design in shadow quilting, select a firm fabric for the backing of the sample, a square of brightly coloured felt slightly larger

Border design taken from a malacate

RIGHT *Quilting a malacate design, with the felt glued in position (at right), the organza overlaying the felt (left above) and quilted in place (left below)*
FAR RIGHT *Reverse image*

Cascacuauhtli (the buzzard) interpreted in shadow quilting

than the motif, a piece of Bondaweb of a similar size, and a larger piece of translucent fabric, preferably organdie or nylon organza.

Trace the design exactly, in reverse, on to the paper side of the sheet of Bondaweb. Remove any excess Bondaweb. Make sure there are no creases in the felt and, having peeled off the protective coating of the Bondaweb, iron it on to the felt. When it is cool, pin the felt, face down, on to a cutting board. Then take a sharp craft knife and cut carefully along the traced lines, being careful not to stretch the felt as you work. Lift each piece carefully and place it, face down, on an ironing board or some other padded surface. Without distorting the shapes, peel off the Bondaweb backing. This is the difficult part of the procedure!

Now lay the backing material over the sticky felt, and press lightly with a damp cloth and an iron hot enough to ensure adhesion.

When it is cool, mount the backing material, plus felt, in an embroidery frame. Lay the

ABOVE LEFT *Flower design from a malacate, with* RIGHT *method in English quilting. Note that the lower half of the 'arrowheads' have been joined to the circle to make the line of quilting more fluid*

RIGHT *Another malacate border in English quilting*

Cushions in English quilting from malacate patterns

BELOW *Malacate border design in canvaswork*

translucent fabric over the design and pin it in place around the outside of the frame, making sure that the grain lines match those of the backing fabric. If they do not match, the work will pucker when released from the frame. Tack in position and remove the pins.

Using a thread that will be invisible against the organza, quilt right up against the edge of the felt, taking care not to catch the edges. Use either stab stitches or back stitches, and keep them as even as possible.

This method of quilting is decorative only. It should not be used for any purpose where it will be subject to wear as it is almost impossible to clean, due to the differing qualities of the fabrics used. Beading could be used along the quilting lines, to accent the design still further.

If you are very careful, and keep all the pieces left over when you cut, you will see that it is possible to make a reverse image (counterchange) of the design.

The civilizations which flourished in what is now Mexico evolved and ebbed for over two thousand years, so it must be appreciated that the few examples given in this chapter are merely to arouse the reader's interest. There are numerous books which illustrate the sculpture, ceramics, paintings and metalwork of these people, whilst many museums have collections worth studying.

CHAPTER TWELVE

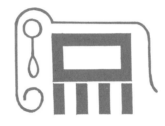

India

What was formerly known as India consists today of Pakistan, Bangladesh and India itself. It is a region of ancient, colourful traditions and a rich cultural and religious diversity.
During this century archaeologists have discovered in the Indus valley in Pakistan the remains of cities belonging to a civilization which flourished for a thousand years from about 2500 years BC. We shall know more about this people when their system of writing has been deciphered, but their relics indicate highly developed artistic capabilities, and a standard of living at least comparable with that of the Roman Empire hundreds of years later.

Steatite seal from Mohenjodaro, third to second millennium BC

Aryan people invaded the Indian sub-continent from the north in about 1500 BC. It is possible that the Dravidians of modern southern India are the descendants of the Indus (or early) people, while the lighter-skinned inhabitants of northern India descend from the Aryan invaders. The Vedas, the great Hindu books, date from this period of conflict and are thought to refer to actual historical events.

Invasions from the north and west continued over the centuries. In the third century BC the Mauryan Empire, under Emperor Ashoka, extended over more of India than was controlled by any other power until the farthest extent of the British conquest in the nineteenth century.

To mark his boundaries Ashoka raised lion-headed pillars, most of which still stand today. The symbol of present-day India is taken from the central boss of these pillars.

Empire succeeded empire for a thousand years. There was continued and extensive trade with the Near East, North Africa and Europe. In AD 52 St Thomas the Apostle is said to have arrived in Kerala in southern India, and to this day there is a strong Christian influence in this region.

The fabled riches of India lured invaders, who included Darius the Persian and Alexander the Great. By AD 1001 Muslim adventurers were venturing over the mountains from Afghanistan,

ABOVE *Lion capital of Ashoka*

RIGHT *Antique sampler, Delhi, using a variety of techniques, including couched gold thread*

ABOVE LEFT *Copy of an Indian embroidery from the Embroiderers' Guild Collection. This goldwork and padded silk sample was worked in the days when copying an historical embroidery in order to understand it better formed part of the City and Guilds of London course.*

ABOVE RIGHT *Peacock in machine embroidery; an attempt to bring the subject up to date*

RIGHT *Three other renditions of the peacock in Indian art and Ganesh, the elephant-headed god of prosperity*

LEFT *Pink sandstone figure from Jamset, Uttar Pradesh, twelfth century AD*

and by 1206 the Sultanate of Delhi had been established, with borders which sometimes extended as far west as Gujarat and as far south as Maharashtra.

In 1527 Babur, a descendant of Genghis Khan, marched into the Punjab and defeated the Sultanate of Delhi at Panipat. With only a brief intermission the Moghul Empire that Babur founded flowered until 1707. A pale shadow of the Moghul Empire continued to exist until the period of British rule, which itself ceased in 1947.

There are so many cultural strands evident in the Indian sub-continent today that it is almost impossible to talk about an 'Indian style'. At the Qutab Minar in Delhi a modern park contains buildings which are a kaleidoscope of Indian cultures and styles. Here the earliest Muslim rulers built a tower of victory and the first mosque in India, using the intricately carved stones of the Hindu temples they had destroyed in order to clear the space. One could happily spend days here collecting designs and puzzling over the date and history of each building.

Each state in India has its own style and particular traditional crafts, from weaving and embroidery to stone carving and gem cutting. The great religions, Hinduism, Buddhism, Sikhism and Islam, have exerted influence as well.

The visitor to India is struck by the colour everywhere, from the dress of the people to the colours of the birds, animals and flowers. The vegetable and spice markets are an inspiration in themselves. Besides motifs based on religious symbols, birds, animals and flowers are well represented in painting, carving and embroidery.

From the sixteenth century onwards painted and embroidered textiles were imported into Europe from the Moghul Empire, and greatly influenced European textiles of the seventeenth and eighteenth centuries. The Jacobean Tree of Life design is taken directly from painted palimpores (bed covers) and embroideries imported from India.

The type of Indian embroidery most frequently found in Western collections is the meticulous chain stitched representations of naturalistic or stylized figures, embroidered on silk or cotton. Surprisingly, these are frequently worked not with a needle but with a handled hook called an ari, rather like a very fine crochet hook. The fabric is mounted in a frame with the thread carried beneath it to be picked up by the ari.

If you want to know whether work has been done in chain stitch or with an ari hook, look at the back of the fabric. Chain stitch will produce a slanted, usually uneven stitch, the ari hook a straight line.

Another type of embroidery which people think of as typically Indian is the mirror work used to embellish clothing, wall hangings and almost any other type of embroidery. The roughly circular pieces of mirror glass are held

Sampler worked in shisha embroidery and chain stitch

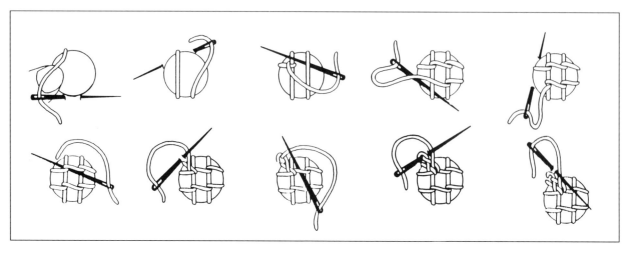

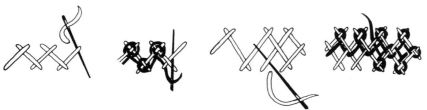

ABOVE *Method of working shisha (mirror) embroidery*
LEFT *Interlaced herringbone stitch*

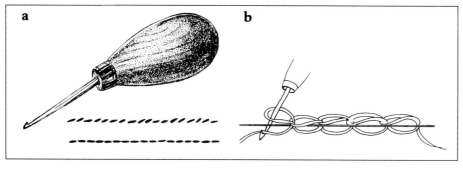

a *Ari hook, showing the reverse side of embroidery worked with an ari (bottom) compared with (top) the reverse side of chain stitched work*
b *Working with an ari hook*

Method of working Maltese cross

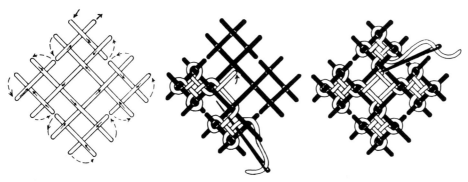

in place by stitching, as shown on p.78, and often further decorated by interlaced herringbone stitch and Maltese cross stitch.

Since this chapter is only a starting point it has had to skim very lightly over the types of embroidery to be found in India. It has not been possible, for instance, to describe the fine wool embroidery from Kashmir, the delicate whitework from Calcutta, or the bold and handsome appliqué from Gujarat with which the local people decorate everything from sun umbrellas to wall hangings. It is all waiting for you to discover in books and museums – or, if you are lucky enough, in India itself.

Cushion embroidered in chain stitch, using a design (much enlarged) from the Moghul robe in the Victoria and Albert Museum, London

Modern table runner from Gujarat, worked with an ari and incorporating some shisha work

CHAPTER THIRTEEN

China

China's chief contribution to the art of embroidery is the discovery of silk, and the development of spinning, weaving and embroidery using this lustrous fibre. Folklore attributes the discovery to Lei-Zu, wife of the legendary Yellow Emperor, who gave it to the women of China; in fact sericulture was probably first practised by Neolithic farmers living near the Yellow River four thousand years ago. The raising of silkworms, the weaving of silk and silk embroidery have traditionally been women's arts in China.

Rubbings taken from carved tiles,
second century AD

The history of China is divided into a series of dynasties, frequently interrupted by periods of civil war or invasion from Central Asia. The first Emperor of whom a detailed account is recorded is Fu-hsi, who is supposed to have ruled from 2852 to 2738 BC. He was followed by other emperors noted for their perfection of character and outstanding abilty as rulers, until, some time in the eighteenth century BC, the Shang dynasty took over.

The discovery of the An-yang tombs has proved that by this time there was already a literate civilization using a script which is recognizably ancestral to modern Chinese characters. Inscribed bronze vessels and intricately carved jade articles survive from that period. The Shang dynasty created a vague tradition of political unity, which subsequent periods of feudal warfare could not completely erase.

ABOVE *Decorated end post of a roof*

ABOVE *Ivory figure of a wise man*

RIGHT *Bird in silk embroidery, worked for the modern tourist trade*

Confucius, who was born in 551 BC, was the first real historian of his country. He gathered up all the traditions of government and conduct handed down through the ages, and welded them into the system of morality which persists in China to this day.

The Chou dynasty came to power after the Shang and continued until 246 BC. Its successors, the Ch'in, expanded the country's borders to take in most of what constitutes modern China, and started the building of the Great Wall.

The Han period, which followed in 202 BC, ranks as one of the country's most prosperous. An excavated Han tomb has revealed a store of well-preserved silk satins, brocades and gauzes, as well as a wardrobe of embroidered robes, using a variety of stitches in addition to the chain stitch which predominated on embroideries found in earlier tombs. This variety of surface stitches required special sewing equipment, and by the Han dynasty needles with eyes, thimbles, and scissors with opposable blades had been developed.

In AD 618 Kao-Tsu made himself the first Emperor of the Tang dynasty. The next three hundred years saw China's borders extended westwards almost to the Caspian Sea and northwards to Korea, while at home ordered government made a propitious home for poets who were honoured as never before. In 960 the Sung dynasty brought in a new era of cultural achievement with the development of printing and the founding of libraries.

Meanwhile Mongol power was increasing. In 1212 Genghis Khan invaded, and continued to press forward into China with his armies until his death in 1227. By the time Kublai Khan came to the throne in 1259 Mongol territory extended from the River Dnieper in the Ukraine to the Pacific in the east, and from the Arctic Ocean to the Straits of Malacca just west of modern Singapore. This period, one of only two periods of foreign rule, is known as the Yuan dynasty.

'Chinese Bird', designed and worked by Joan Fowler

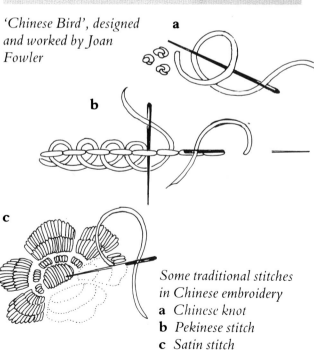

Some traditional stitches in Chinese embroidery
a *Chinese knot*
b *Pekinese stitch*
c *Satin stitch*

In 1368 a native leader expelled the Mongols from Peking and started the Ming dynasty, noted more for the arts of peace than those of war. Under the Mings there was considerable trade with Europe and Africa, particularly through the port of Canton, and Christian missionaries were allowed to enter the country with the European traders.

In 1616 a force of Manchu Tartars invaded China and captured Liaotung. It was not long before they had gained control of the whole country, introducing the last great dynasty, the Manchus.

In the nineteenth century the European powers, who until then had traded amicably enough with China, decided they wanted more advantageous arrangements and carried on a series of minor wars, assisted considerably by weak and unstable Chinese governments. The Manchu dynasty fell in the early twentieth century, leaving China open to foreign exploitation and Japanese invasion.

There are four principal traditional embroidery centres in China. Weaving and embroidery were first established in Szechwan over 1500 years ago. The work from this region consists mainly of lavishly embroidered

Borders from Chinese porcelain

Dragon from Chinese embroidery

Chinese horse from the Tang dynasty

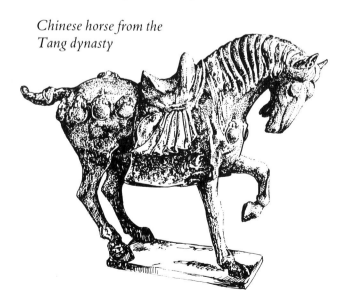

Various ways of representing the character shou, *meaning long life*

Ying and yang, the symbol expressing perfect balance

kimonos for the Japanese market, and simpler work on household goods.

Hunan embroidery specializes in realistic renditions of animals and landscapes, using hair-thin silk or even human hair. The Kwangtung style, at its peak during the Tang and Ming dynasties, is more ornate. A considerable quantity of gold, pearls and precious stones is used, and the work often incorporates peacock feathers.

Soochow, in the heart of the silk-producing country, has been the centre of silk weaving and embroidery for centuries. Found here are the double-sided pictures worked on gauze which confound European embroiderers.

A handkerchief brought back from China in 1992

Other treatments of flowers in Chinese embroidery

*An attempt at copying Chinese satin stitch embroidery
in order to understand the technique better*

*Butterflies and moths
from Chinese embroidery*

*Method of working
double-sided satin stitch*

CHAPTER FOURTEEN

Japan

No one is quite certain where the Japanese people originated. Before the Emperor Jimmu (reputed to be the first mortal ruler) came to the throne in 660 BC, they had no written records. While some authorities assume that the Ainu people, who now inhabit a few areas of northern Japan, were the original inhabitants and were conquered by immigrants from Korea and China, there is now little chance of the early history of the Japanese islands being discovered.

Fish in a typical Japanese interpretation of water

By about AD 500 the erstwhile warring peoples of Japan had become one nation, a mixture of Ainu, Mongols and peoples from southern Asia. Buddhism had been introduced from the Asian mainland, becoming the official religion by 562. The government was headed by the Emperor, who ruled through powerful lords from three principal families. In time the power of the Emperor became almost totally eroded, leaving him as a figurehead. Over the centuries a kind of feudal system evolved. Power shifted between the governing and the military classes, and was occasionally taken over by a particularly enterprising emperor.

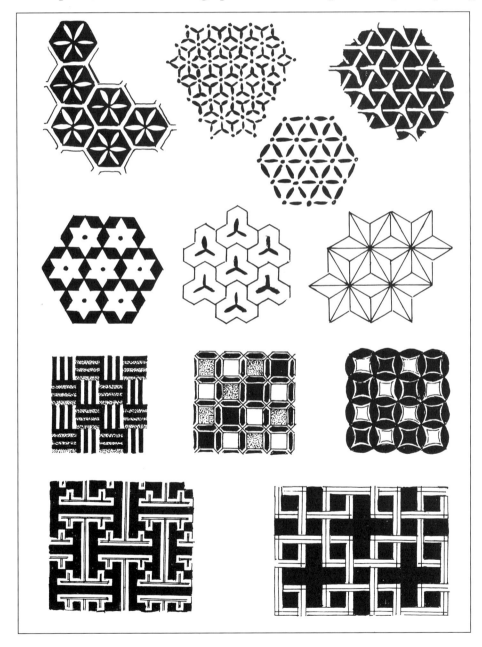

Japanese dress from a nineteenth-century woodcut. Several layers of kimono were worn, one over the other, for decoration and, when necessary, for warmth

Designs from cloisonné enamels, based on hexagons, squares and circles

There was always considerable cultural interchange between China and Japan, and a number of Chinese words have been taken into the various Japanese languages. Trade with Europeans did not get under way until the sixteenth century, when the Portuguese and Dutch established trading posts. The Portuguese introduced first Jesuit missionaries, then Franciscans, in an attempt to convert the Japanese, who followed a form of Buddhism known as Shinto. Unfortunately, Franciscans and Jesuits warred against each other so much that they disgusted the Japanese, who threw out all Europeans, including the Protestant Dutch. Converts who refused to renounce their new Christian religion, which the Japanese believed to be merciless and fanatical, were exterminated.

Trade with the West was not resumed until an American naval officer, Commodore Perry, visited and obtained a trading agreement in the 1850s. This opened the way for the Russians and the British. The rigid social regime which had changed very little over the centuries made it easy for the military classes in Japan to embroil the country in wars of aggression, some of which, like that against Russia in 1905, were very successful. Not until Japan's defeat by the Allies in 1945 at the end of the Second World War, and the subsequent occupation of the chain of islands, was a democratic style of government adopted.

Japanese art is realistic, aiming at perfection, but dismissing the non-essential. This approach is seen in all media, from inlay work on bronze, to the carving of the tiny figures known as netsuke out of wood and ivory; their skill in the field of textiles, whether woven, printed or embroidered, is unmatched.

The crests of the Shoguns, the Japanese noblemen, were interpreted in metal and ivory, and also embroidered on clothing as spot motifs, interspersed with more naturalistic renditions of plants and animals. The embroidery was mostly executed in silk thread on silk fabric, with some gold work.

Designs for Shashiko embroidery, traditionally used on the short cotton coats of Japanese workers

JAPAN

RIGHT *Brooch, based on a badge, worked in felt and silk threads*

BELOW *Crane, adapted from a badge design, worked in silk*

An assortment of badges adopted by Japanese nobles, roughly equating with European armorial bearings

This lavish decoration was reserved for the ruling classes. The working people were not allowed to wear silk, and made their clothing instead from cotton, linen or hempen fabrics. They decorated their garments with quilting stitches in a contrasting colour, using fairly coarse, but even, running stitches. Generally such fabrics were dyed blue with indigo, and were stitched in white, but other contrasting colours can look just as effective.

An appreciation of nature is part of the Japanese culture. Interpretations of flowers, landscape and gardens appear in all media, from painting to cloisonné enamel and lacquer.

Despite the revolution in their way of life since 1945, the Japanese have retained their respect for the traditional decorative arts and continue to practise them. Traditional dress is still worn on special occasions, while embroidery is used on screens and pictures for decoration of the home.

Unlike China, Japan has always reserved embroidery as work for men. It is only recently that the skills were taught to women as well.

Japanese plant and garden images

JAPAN

Badge in brass with
champlevé enamel

Panel in 'inexpensive gold work', inspired by
Hokusai's famous wood engraving The Wave

Designs from sword hilts

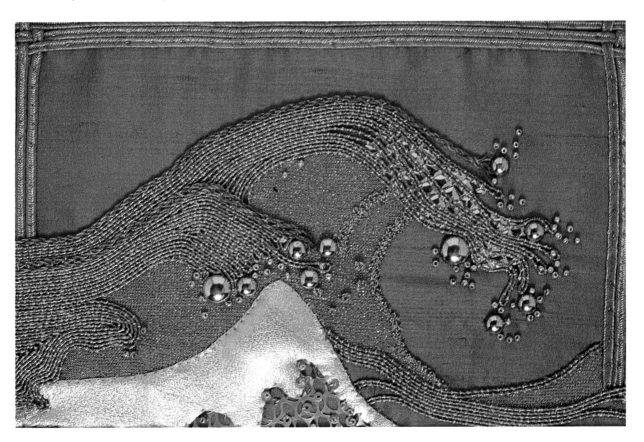

93

CHAPTER FIFTEEN

Africa

The name 'Africa' was first given by the Romans to their provinces south of the Mediterranean and west of the Red Sea. The name has since been extended to include the whole continent, which the Greeks and Romans had called Libya.

The first record of circumnavigation of the continent was reported by the Greek historian Herodotus (485–425 BC). According to him, Necho, King of Egypt (610–594 BC) sailed down the Red Sea and returned, three years later, via the Straits of Gibraltar and the Mediterranean. Despite this pioneering voyage, the greater part of Africa remained a mystery, however, and even the Arab geographers of the seventh century did not venture farther than the dry lands south of the Sahara.

Large ivory carving, studded with copper spots as decoration

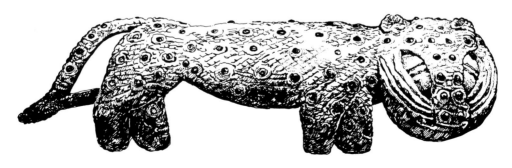

Although there was Arab trade with the east coast, the Atlantic shores of Africa remained virtually unexplored until the Portuguese ventured south in the fifteenth century. Bartholomeu Diaz discovered the Cape of Good Hope at the southernmost tip of the continent in 1487, and ten years later Vasco da Gama discovered the Cape route to India. These discoveries opened up Africa to exploration, trade and exploitation in the next three centuries, the chief trade goods being slaves for the American colonies and gold.

The immense landmass of Africa is sparsely populated, compared with Europe, largely because of the climate and vegetation. The dry lands south of the Sahara sustain only a meagre population; the central rain forests are almost equally unfriendly to human life. Only the savannahs of east and southern Africa are capable of supporting a considerable population.

It is now generally accepted that human beings evolved in East Africa, but there is little evidence to tell us anything about them. The indigenous races found by the advancing Europeans fell into three main categories: the Semitic peoples of East Africa who had presumably come from Egypt and the Arabian peninsula; the Negroes who spread eastwards and southwards from West Africa, through present-day Kenya and Uganda and down to the Cape; and the light-skinned, cattle-rearing, migratory Hottentots who roamed the south-western coastal districts.

North of the Sahara the people are mostly Muslims and have been discussed in Chapter 8. The ancient Egyptian civilization has been described in Chapter 3. Although this leaves a huge geographical area to be treated in this chapter, in some Western countries documentation on African art tends to be scarce and museum collections meagre.

Pre-Muslim and pre-Christian religions in Africa appear to have been largely animist – their followers believed that God existed in all

Decorated African pot

Stylized rendition of a hippopotamus

forms of nature. Some of the earliest artefacts to interest modern Europeans were tribal masks, which were collected and exhibited in the West in the late nineteenth and early twentieth centuries, providing inspiration for Cubist painters and sculptors such as the young Picasso.

Fabrics in Africa are decorated by tie-dyeing, printing and embroidery. The patterns used are most frequently geometrical.

95

Ivory wrist band from Benin

Panel in silk and suede, worked in appliqué and machine embroidery, using the patterns from raffia fabrics from Zaire as background

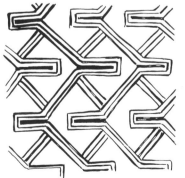

The Empire of Benin in West Africa was founded about AD 900 and continued with fluctuating prosperity until it was destroyed by the British in 1897. In the fifteenth century it had reached the height of its power and prosperity, becoming a centre for the trade in ivory, pepper, cloth, metal, beads and slaves. It is particularly well known today because of the skill of its ivory carvers and its cast bronzes.

Bronze head from Benin

Mask from Zaire, with fur 'horns' and a raffia costume

Bangwa memorial figure, collected in Cameroon in the nineteenth century

LEFT *Whitework (drawn work and cutwork as well as surface stitchery and beading) laid over a Lurex background. This is a translation of a Benin portrait in ivory*

Nimba mask from Guinea

Gu mask from Baule, with OPPOSITE *a modern mask in leather and gold based on it*

CHAPTER SIXTEEN

Australia and New Zealand

When European travellers first landed in Australia in the late eighteenth century they were met by the aboriginal inhabitants of the continent. These appeared to be a distinct species of the human race, tall, dark-skinned and wiry, with tight, curly hair. In their tribal state they were one of the most primitive people in existence – although they possessed a complex social organization, they had no knowledge of metals or agriculture. The aborigines lived a nomadic life, wandering in search of game and edible vegetation. It is now believed that they originally came from the Malay peninsula, but in the very distant past.

Magpie geese, from a painting by George Mulpurrurru

Interpretation of a salt-water crocodile based on a painting by Roy Link. Worked in appliqué, couching and French knots

Design based on an aborigine painting, to be interpreted in three colours in rug hooking or chain stitch

Until quite recent times neither their art nor their way of life was appreciated by the European settlers. The population fell dramatically from the estimated three hundred thousand at the time of Cook's discovery to the fifty thousand or so full-blooded aborigines left today.

The early Australians lacked a written language but had a very rich oral tradition based on myth and legend. Most of their paintings interpret these myths or are based on pure pattern. Designs believed to be up to sixty thousand years old have been found on the walls of rocks and caves which the aborigines hold sacred.

Most aborigine art consisted of sand paintings, paintings on bark with earth colours, and in body painting; as a result, few examples survived for long. Today, however, quite a number of talented aborigines have translated their traditional designs into painting in oil and acrylic. A favourite technique involves laying in a background of flat colour (representing the basic colour of sand or bark) and then painting on to this with a series of round dots, building up a pattern. This technique begs to be interpreted in French knots, or to be translated into rug hooking patterns.

Because they did not practise agriculture, Australian aborigines did not spin or weave plant or animal fibres so they have no tradition of textile art.

Detail from a painting in the Pitt Rivers Museum, Oxford, showing stylized human figures

Drawings on sandstone, thought to be 60,000 years old, in Arnhem Land

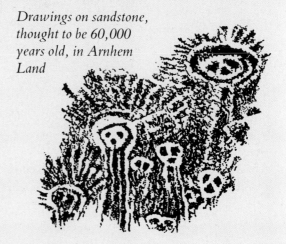

The natives of New Zealand are of quite a different physical type. Racially they are Caucasoid, and, with their olive skin and facial features not unlike those of some Europeans, were more easily accepted as equals by the Europeans than were the aborigines of Australia. The once universal practice of tattooing the faces of men and women with swirling patterns has now largely ceased.

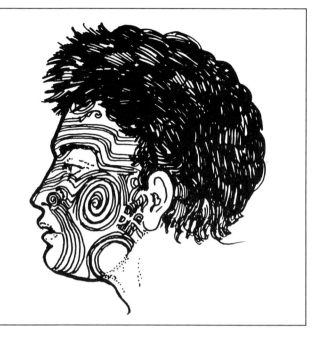

Maori tattooing, based on a drawing by a European traveller in 1833

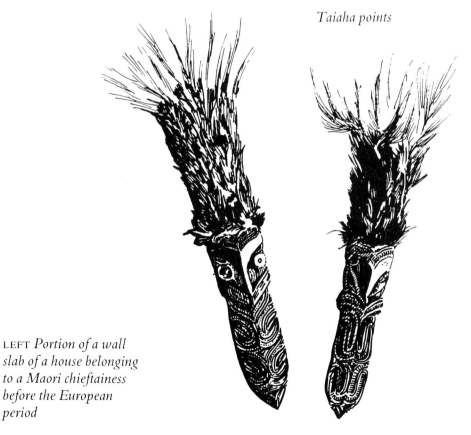

Taiaha points

LEFT *Portion of a wall slab of a house belonging to a Maori chieftainess before the European period*

The name 'Maori' means 'indigenous people', and was the name the natives of New Zealand gave themselves. They were an advanced Neolithic civilization when discovered by European explorers in the eighteenth century. Maori legends suggest that they colonized New Zealand from the Pacific islands.

The Maoris were expert carvers. Before the Europeans came they used tools made from the local greenstone, but once they acquired metal knives their carving skills were much more readily employed. Maori carvings of the human form are stylized. Often the head is much enlarged, so that special care can be devoted to the correct tattoo patterns on the face. Carving was used on many articles in everyday use, from implements of agriculture, hunting and fishing to weapons of war. The taiaha was a weapon, but was also used as a staff of office when addressing an assembly. The taiaha points illustrated on p.103 show how the human tongue is enlarged to show defiance, while above it are shown the upper lip, eyes and forehead.

Many Maoris have now become Christian, but before the influx of Europeans their religion was based on the Sky Father and Earth Mother and a mythological population of spirits. One figure which appears frequently in Maori carvings is the manaia, which is best described as a side-faced figure, sometimes humanistic, sometimes birdlike. Modern Maoris describe it as a spirit, with the inference that it is menacing rather than friendly. Manaias traditionally have some or all of these features: something of a body, a head with an eye and a beak, a shoulder, an arm, a three-fingered hand and a leg with three toes. The spirits are frequently depicted in such a stylized form that they are difficult to recognize.

The illustrations here may whet your appetite to look for further sources of inspiration in Maori tribal artefacts. Unfortunately, however, it appears that compared, say, to the Indians of the Pacific coast of the United States and Canada, little has been published on Maori design.

OPPOSITE *A treasure box or paphou used to keep small trinkets or amulets*

BELOW *Manaia figure interpreted in blackwork stitches in fine gold thread and surface embroidery in wool. The idea was to show a cloudlike spirit obscuring a portion of the temperate rain forest in New Zealand*

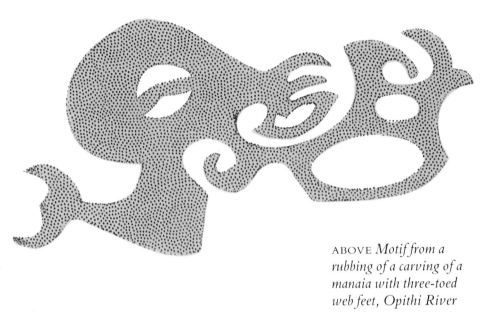

ABOVE *Motif from a rubbing of a carving of a manaia with three-toed web feet, Opithi River*

CHAPTER SEVENTEEN

The Indians of the Pacific Coast

When in 1778 Captain James Cook explored the islands and inlets of what is now British Columbia and Alaska in the vain search for the western end of the Northwest Passage, he encountered several tribes of 'Indians' who lived on the narrow strips of land between the ocean and the unwelcoming mountains. Other explorers and fur traders had made contact with these tribes before, but this was the first time that detailed records were made, and numerous artefacts were brought back to Britain for study.

Fish design from the Queen Charlotte Islands

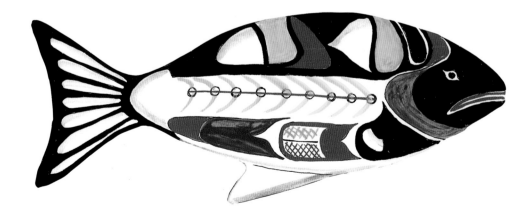

These 'Indians' – the Tlingit in the north, the Haida of the Queen Charlotte Islands, the Tsimshian, Bella Coola and Kwakiutl of the centre, the Nootka of Vancouver Island, and the Salish of what is now the US state of Washington – were largely dependent for their livelihood on fishing and hunting. They had no creation myth, but believed that from the beginning the world was inhabited by the 'Original People' from whom all life descended. Thus they claimed cousinship with the raven, the hawk, the bear, the dogfish, the salmon and all living creatures, as well as the sun, moon and stars, the wind and the rain. Each family had a totem creature and used a stylized representation of it to adorn their houses, their clothing, their ritual masks, their drums and their simple furniture.

RIGHT, ABOVE AND BELOW *Tote bags based on designs from the Pacific North-west*

BELOW *Ancestral mask of the Bella Coola Indians*

Haida totem poles in the
Queen Charlotte Islands

Best known are the totem poles which they erected in front of their houses, examples of which have found their way into museums all over the world. These told the history of the family and could be loosely compared to a European coat of arms with quarterings. Similar designs were carved into and painted on door posts, seats, storage boxes, weapons and tools, as well as many fabulous ceremonial masks. Almost all carving was in wood – cedar was readily available and easy to work. Colours were flat and basic – black, red and white with some yellow and blue, leaving the reddish cedar wood or golden spruce root as background.

When the early explorers tried to lure the Indians into exchanging their furs for trade goods it was difficult to arouse interest. These independent people dressed in furs or cured skins, and wove hats, baskets, cloaks and blankets out of spruce root, or a combination of spruce root and goat hair. Unhappily, after the diseases introduced by Europeans (more or less accidentally) had decimated the population and largely destroyed their culture, they became dependent upon trade and old skills were lost. Now, instead of weaving the designs into the blankets they prized, or painting them on, they appliquéd one colour (usually red) on to black trade blankets and outlined or emphasized the patterns with shell or, later, mother of pearl buttons.

RIGHT *Traditional Chilkat cloak woven of commercial wool. In former times these would have been of dog and/or goat hair*

BELOW *'The Raven Eating the Sun', an explanation of the eclipse. Canvaswork with beads*

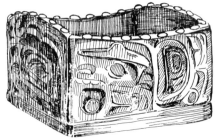

LEFT TO RIGHT
*Southern Kwakiutl
mask, Haida bentwood
bowl, Haida carved
wooden bowl, featuring
both a whale and an
eagle*

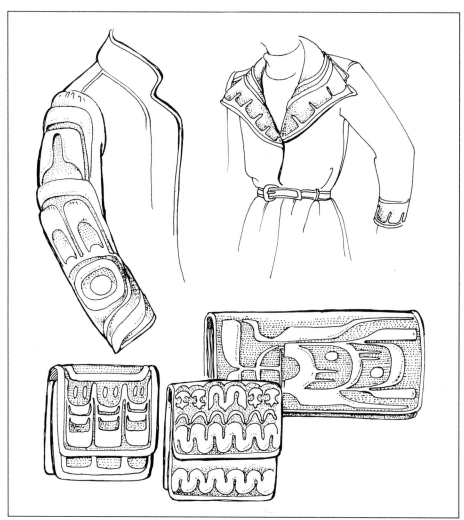

*Decoration for clothing
and bags, based on these
designs*

During the past fifty years there has been a conscious and reasonably successful attempt to recapture the skills of the past and reclaim the former culture. Tribal artists are working in traditional materials and in stone and precious metals, interpreting the almost forgotten symbols.

As well as the ceremonial masks which were part of their rituals, the Indians decorated the utensils they used for cooking and eating, as well as their houses and their boats. On ceremonial occasions the chief would sit on a kind of settee decorated with his crests.

One outstanding invention of the coastal Indians was the bentwood bowl or box. A strip of cedar was split away from the log by the use of adzes and a hammer. It was adzed smooth to the desired thickness, and then three equidistant grooves, at right-angles to the board, were made with a sharp knife.

The board was now placed on a bed of wet seaweed over a pit of coals, covered with wet seaweed and steamed. As the wood softened, the maker bent the board into right-angles along the grooves, forming a four-sided box. Holes were drilled along the joined edges and the two ends were sewn together with rootlets of spruce. A bottom section was cut to fit and pinned in place. The exterior was then incised and painted or carved.

ABOVE *Haida ceremonial robe. Trade goods blanket, red on black, with decoration of abalone shell, white shell beads and mother of pearl buttons*

RIGHT *Hat woven from spruce root, and painted with a design based on the mountain goat*

LEFT *Cradle woven from spruce root. As the Haida are matrilineal, the dogfish crest is that of the mother*

CHAPTER EIGHTEEN

Art Nouveau

The Art Nouveau style developed in Europe towards the end of the nineteenth century and flowered in the first decade of the twentieth. It was effectively halted by the First World War.

Art Nouveau rejected the Classical heritage which had dominated Europe for centuries since the Renaissance, and sought inspiration in other civilizations, particularly those of Assyria, Egypt and the Far East. The Catalan architect Antonio Gaudi, one of the earliest exponents of the style, claimed that the Renaissance had debased and destroyed the emerging Gothic style of the Middle Ages; Gaudi proclaimed his wish that he might 'continue the Gothic, not reproduce or imitate it.' In Britain the Pre-Raphaelite Brotherhood pursued a similar line, seeking to go back before the Renaissance for their inspiration.

Moth brooch by C. R. Ashbee

Some of the early German practitioners of Art Nouveau based their work on Rococo decoration, with its soft, organic curves. Japanese art, newly available in Europe, also exerted a very strong influence. Whilst illuminated Celtic manuscripts with their unity of decoration and typography, and the calligraphy and intricate designs from Islamic art, also played their part, the artists and craftsmen rarely based their new style directly upon older sources but used them as a starting point to design something new. The ideal was to capture the spirit of the original without disclosing the source. Above all, plant and animal forms were used as inspiration, though never copied slavishly, with the artist abstracting the shapes rather than 'counterfeiting nature'.

ABCDEFGHIJKLM
NOPQRSTUV
WXYZ

One of the many Art Nouveau alphabets

Copper wall sconce by Marian Wilson, Glasgow

Tiffany vase, 1895

Motif from 'La Plume' calendar by Mucha

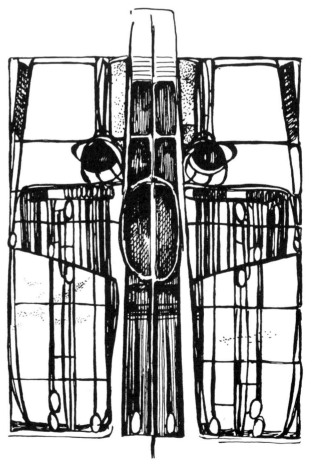

Doors from the Willow Tea Rooms in Glasgow, designed by Charles Rennie Mackintosh

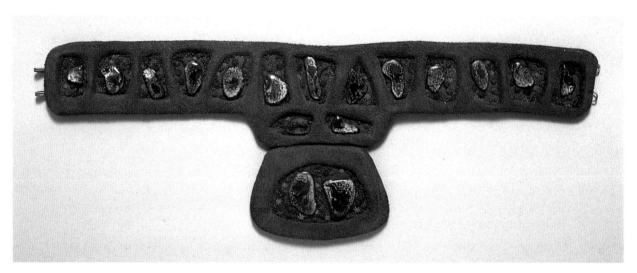

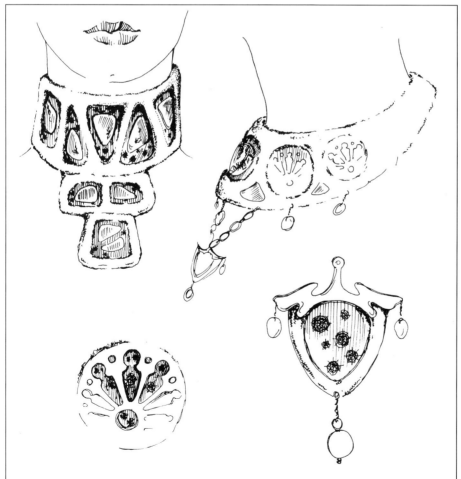

ABOVE *Neck ornament in suede, embroidery and enamel, based on a study of Art Nouveau embroidery, with* BELOW *studies for this piece*

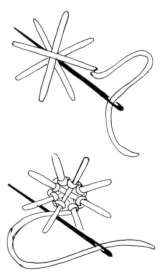

ABOVE *Design for embroidery based on* BELOW *the tiled facade of the Majolikahaus in Vienna, built by Otto Wagner in 1898*

For thirty years or so the Style was popular throughout Europe and North America, whether known as Jugendstil in Germany, Le Style Moderne in France, Sezession in Austria, Stile Liberty in Italy, Modernista in Spain or Art Nouveau in Britain and America. Its popularity was enhanced by the proliferation of art and craft periodicals illustrated by the newly developed photographic processes, which introduced it to a wide audience, whilst examples of articles in the Art Nouveau style were made available to a wide market by cheap methods of reproduction.

Unlike the Pre-Raphaelites, practitioners of Art Nouveau eagerly made use of machinery in the production of their work. C. F. A. Voysey, one of the leading designers in the Art Nouveau style in Britain, insisted that one must live and work in the present and not hark back to techniques and methods of earlier times.

If the design were to be used for a cushion, velvet stitch could be useful for the flower forms

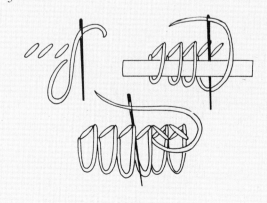

ABOVE *Small panel in silk and gold based on Gustav Klimt's paintings*

For the first time since the Middle Ages the artificial demarcation between 'Fine Art' painters and craftsmen was erased, with painters such as Pierre Bonnard and Edouard Vuillard designing stained glass windows for Tiffany and painting murals and theatre sets, and Henri Van de Velde in Belgium giving up a promising career as a painter to devote his time to designing tapestries, metalwork, wallpaper and furniture. Poster making was elevated into the realms of fine art by painters such as Alphonse Mucha, Toulouse-Lautrec and Bonnard.

Basically, there were two types of design. The curvilinear, whiplash form, based on or abstracted from natural forms, was seen particularly in the work of French and Belgian artists, such as Hector Guimard's designs for the Paris Metro. The geometrical style, typified by many of the Vienna Sezession artists and the Scottish architect and designer Charles Rennie Mackintosh, owed much of its inspiration to Japanese design. The objects resulting from either source were likely to be asymmetrical, and could well combine both influences.

There was an implicit eroticism in much of the work, particularly in the jewellery, although the posters of Toulouse-Lautrec and Mucha and the drawings of Aubrey Beardsley carried this tendency even further. For embroiderers the painter who provided the most fertile source of inspiration was Gustav Klimt.

BELOW *Wall hanging
based on a detail from
Klimt's panel* Die
Erfüllung *(Fulfilment).
The base material is silk
noile (a rather rough,
firm fabric), with
appliqué in various fine
leathers, using beads and
gold work as well as
embroidery stitches for
decoration*

CHAPTER NINETEEN

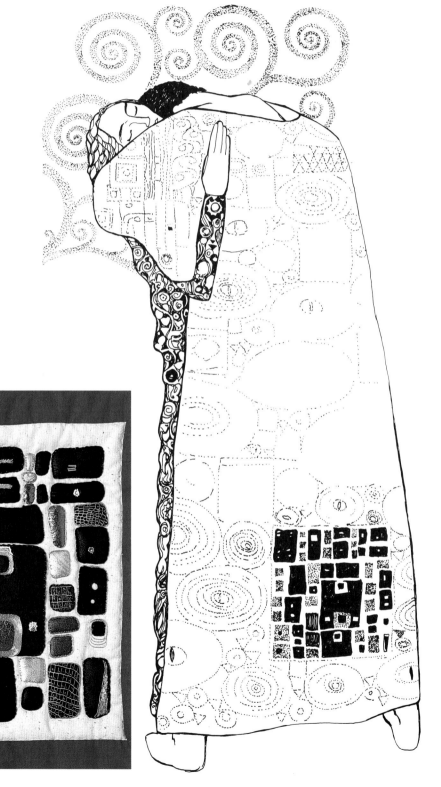

Art Deco

Although the term 'Art Deco' was not in universal use until the 1960s, the style was launched at the Exposition Nationale des Arts Décoratifs et Industriels Modernes in Paris in 1925. Its 'modern' style persisted until the New York World's Fair of 1939–40, and finally expired with the Second World War.
The geometrical forms and the stylized flower, animal and human figures grew out of the simplicity of Art Nouveau. However, where examples of the latter were inclined to be lovingly hand crafted, Art Deco designs tended to be designed for mass production.

Pottery by Clarice Cliff

Art Deco has many sources: African tribal art, Central American architecture and Egyptian art all played their part. The sets and costumes of the Ballets Russes were an influence, and the paintings of the Fauves, the Cubists and the Constructivists had a profound effect.

It was an era in which lifestyles had to be streamlined. There were few servants, as only the very rich could afford them, and women who had found a new independence working in industry during the First World War were not inclined to return to such restrictive

Panel based on a jug designed by Clarice Cliff and worked in satin stitch and chain stitch. It is astonishing how dated the designs of our grandmothers' days look to us now

Trylon and Perisphere, cheap plastic souvenirs from the New York World's Fair, 1939

119

employment. More women went out of the home to work, and smaller, more convenient, houses were built, easier to run than those of previous eras, when servants had been available even to those of relatively modest means. With the general availability of electricity and gas, the new cookers, irons and vacuum cleaners all made housework less onerous.

Mass-produced radio set, 1938

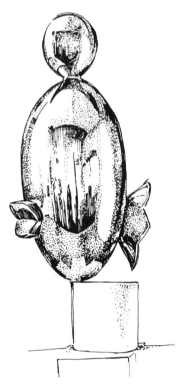

Samples from Art Deco alphabets

La Négresse Blonde, 1932, sculpture by Constantin Brancusi

Bookbinding by Rose Adler for Colette's classic novel Chéri

Two enamelled vases by Camille Faure

Furnishings, fabrics and ceramics followed the new mode, using new materials. Synthetic fabrics came on the market and plastics were used where wood or metal would have been chosen in the past. With mass production, and cheaper materials, fashionable goods became available to a much larger proportion of the population than ever before.

Artist-craftsmen who in previous decades would have made single items, or had their designs copied in a small workshop for the privileged few, became responsible for goods produced in thousands rather than single figures. Although designers such as Susie Cooper and Clarice Cliff made ceramics for the mass market, their work is now much sought after.

Lid of powder compact produced for the mass trade

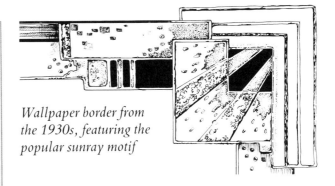

Wallpaper border from the 1930s, featuring the popular sunray motif

Woollen carpet, American, 1930s

Design from a Faure vase, with cushion cover worked from that design in machine appliqué

RIGHT *and* OPPOSITE
Various renditions of the female face

Stained glass window by Jacques Gruber

Carved alabaster head by
Georges Coste

French fashion
illustration

RIGHT *Art Deco lady,*
designed and worked by
Joan Rodwell

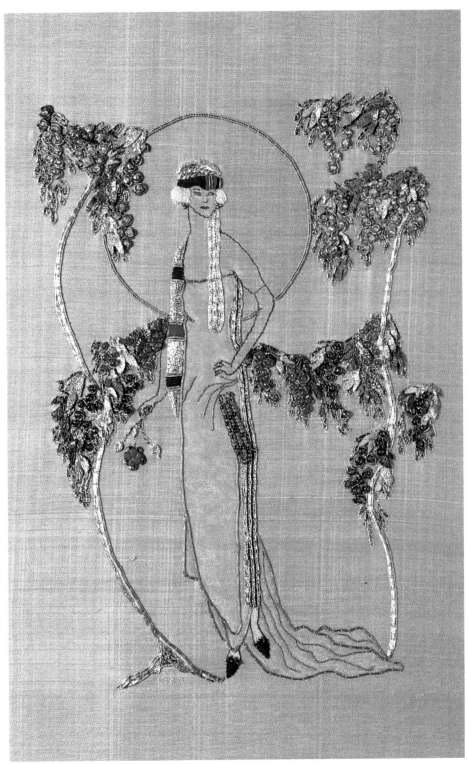

Further Reading and Museums

FURTHER READING

This book is intended to be a general overview of some of the huge range of historical, cultural and geographical sources available to the embroiderer. If you wish to delve deeper into any of these areas, here is a list of books which I found useful in my research.

AUBREY, GEORGE AND CUTLER, THOMAS, *The Grammar of Japanese Ornament*, Studio Editions, 1989

BAIN, GEORGE, *Celtic Art – The Methods of Construction*, Constable, 1987

BAYER, PATRICIA, *Art Deco Source Book*, Phaidon, 1989

BOLTER, MICHAEL, *The Art of Utopia – A New Direction in Contemporary Aboriginal Art*, Craftsmans House, 1992

ENCISO, JORGE, *Designs from Pre-Columbian Mexico*, Dover, 1971

EZRA, KATE, *The Royal Art of Benin – the Perls Collection*, Metropolitan Museum, New York, 1992

GILLOW, JOHN AND BARNARD, NICHOLAS, *Traditional Indian Textiles*, Thames and Hudson, 1991

HASLAM, MALCOLM, *In the Nouveau Style*, Thames and Hudson, 1989

HAWTHORN, AUDREY, *Kwakiutl Art*, University of Washington Press, 1979

HUNT, NORMAN BANCROFT AND FORMAN, WERNER, *People of the Totem*, Peter Bedrick Books, New York, 1989

JONES, OWEN, *The Grammar of Chinese Ornament*, Studio Editions, 1988

JONES, OWEN, *The Grammar of Ornament*, Studio Editions, 1986

Larousse Encyclopaedia of Ancient and Medieval History, Paul Hamlyn, 1965

MACNAIR, PETER, HOOVER, ALAN L. AND NEARY, KEVIN *The Legacy: Tradition and Innovation in Northwest Indian Art*, University of Washington Press, 1984

SCHELE/MILLER, *The Blood of Kings: Dynasty and Ritual in Maya Art*, Thames and Hudson, 1987

SPELTZ, A., *The History of Ornament*, Studio Editions, 1989

SPELTZ, A., *The Styles of Ornament*, Dover, 1959

A good general book on needlecraft:
EMBROIDERER'S GUILD PRACTICAL STUDY GROUP, *Needlework School*, Windward Press, 1985

MUSEUMS

The following museums contain excellent historical and/or ethnographical collections:

Australia

Australian Museum, Sydney
Australian National Gallery, Canberra
South Australian Museum, Adelaide

Austria

Kunsthistorisches Museum, Vienna

Canada

Royal Ontario Museum, Toronto
Museum of Anthropology, Vancouver

France

Musée des Arts Décoratifs, Paris
Musée du Louvre, Paris

Germany

Pergamon Museum, Berlin

Great Britain

Ashmolean Museum, Oxford
British Museum, London
Fitzwilliam Museum, Cambridge
Horniman Museum, London
Museum of Mankind, London
Pitt Rivers Museum, Oxford
Royal Museum of Scotland, Edinburgh
Victoria and Albert Museum, London

Holland

Rijksmuseum, Amsterdam

Italy

Vatican Museums, Rome
Bargello, Florence

Russia

Hermitage, St Petersburg

South Africa

Africana Museum in Progress, Johannesburg
National Cultural History Museum, Pretoria

Spain

Archaeological Museum, Seville
Archaeological Museum, Córdoba
National Museum of Roman Art, Mérida
National Archaeological Museum, Madrid

USA

Museum of Fine Arts, Boston
National Gallery of Art, Washington DC
Metropolitan Museum of Art, New York
Smithsonian Institution, Washington DC

Index

Page numbers in *italic* refer to illustrations